Working with refugee children

Working with refugee children

Jill Rutter

JR
JOSEPH
ROWNTREE
FOUNDATION

Joseph Rowntree Foundation
The Homestead
40 Water End
York YO30 6WP
Website: www.jrf.org.uk

© London Metropolitan University 2003

First published 2003 by the Joseph Rowntree Foundation

ISBN 1 85935 138 7 (paperback)
ISBN 1 85935 139 5 (pdf: available at www.jrf.org.uk)

Prepared and printed by:
York Publishing Services Ltd
64 Hallfield Road
Layerthorpe
York YO31 7ZQ
Tel: 01904 430033; Fax: 01904 430868; Website: www.yps-publishing.co.uk

Further copies of this report, or any other JRF publication, can be obtained either from the JRF website (www.jrf.org.uk/bookshop/) or from our distributor, York Publishing Services Ltd, at the above address.

Contents

1 Introduction

There are over 18 million refugees in today's world and the migration of refugees is a growing challenge to governments and non-governmental organisations alike. Although most refugee children live in poor countries there are probably over 120,000 asylum-seeking and refugee children in the UK. This report focuses on asylum-seeking and refugee children under the age of eight (there is a much smaller body of literature about this group than older refugee children). In particular, the report examines their welfare and educational needs, and responses to these needs. It also highlight gaps in knowledge about young refugee children.

Refugee children in the UK: terminology and human rights instruments

The term 'asylum-seeker' and 'refugee' are used throughout this report and both have a specific legal meaning. An asylum-seeker is someone who has crossed an international border in search of safety, and refugee status, in another country. To be recognised as having refugee status, a person must have left his or her own country or be unable to return to it 'owing to a well-founded fear of being persecuted for reasons of race, religion, nationality, membership of a particular social group or political opinion.' (From the 1951 UN Convention Relating to the Status of Refugees.)

The 1951 UN Convention Relating to the Status of Refugees and its 1967 Protocol are the two international legal instruments that determine the rights of asylum-seekers and refugees. Other human rights instruments have bearings on asylum-seeking and refugee children. The 1989 UN Convention on the Rights of the Child enshrines children's rights, including:

- the right to judgements by the judiciary, welfare agencies and government that are taken in the best interests of the child (Article 3)

- the right to family unity and reunion (Article 10)

- protection of children without families (Article 20)

- ensuring that asylum-seeking and refugee children receive protection and assistance (Article 22)

- the right to liberty (Article 37).

It is frequently argued that aspects of the UK's treatment of asylum-seeking children contravene the spirit of the Convention on the Rights of the Child. Indeed, NGOs often highlight this in lobbying the UN. However, the UK has acceded to the

Convention on the Rights of the Child with reservations, namely that children subject to immigration control, including asylum-seeking children, are excluded from rights that the Convention enshrines.

Applying for asylum

Asylum applications can be lodged at the port of entry or 'in-country' after arrival. Many of those who lodge asylum applications in-country have arrived as clandestine entrants to the UK. The closing of legal routes of entry to the European Union has meant that in the last decade greater proportions of asylum-seekers have been forced to use the services of traffickers to enter the EU. Families may take great risks to enter the EU, and there have been continued reports of deaths en route, including of young children.

In order to make an asylum application, the primary asylum applicant has to recount details of past persecution to the Immigration and Nationality Directorate (IND), part of the Home Office. On the basis of information given to the IND, a decision is made on the asylum-seeker's case. After full consideration of a case, there may be one of four outcomes:

- Refugee Status (10 per cent of decisions in 2003) (Home Office, 2002a). Refugee status protects a person from being returned to his or her country of origin and confers other rights, such as the right to bring immediate family into the UK, the right to work and the right to most of the benefits of a British subject.

- Humanitarian Protection. This is a new immigration status introduced in April 2003. It is granted to asylum-seekers refused refugee status, who, if returned to their country of origin would face a serious risk to life from one or more of the following reasons: the death penalty, unlawful killing, torture, inhuman or degrading treatment or punishment. Those who receive Humanitarian Protection usually receive it for a period of three years.

- Discretionary Leave. This is granted by the Home Secretary outside the provisions of the Immigration Rules. It is granted to people refused asylum who cannot be returned to their home country, or a safe third country. It is also granted to some unaccompanied children who cannot be legally returned home until they are 18.

  In April 2003, Humanitarian Protection and Discretionary Leave replaced the status of Exceptional Leave to Remain (ELR). Throughout the 1980s and 1990s most asylum-seekers who were allowed to stay in the UK, received ELR.

- Refusal (accounting for 66 per cent of decisions after full consideration in 2002). Asylum-seekers may be rejected without a full consideration of their case, at the port of entry after an application has been judged to be 'manifestly unfounded'. Asylum-seekers can also be rejected for 'non-compliance' – failure to attend interviews or failure to return application forms to the Home Office within tight deadlines. Some 18 per cent of all decisions made in 2001 were rejections for non-compliance. Asylum-seekers may be rejected after full consideration of their cases. Once an asylum application has been refused, the applicant can appeal, leave the UK voluntarily, be removed or choose to 'disappear'. Some 20–30 per cent of appeals are usually successful.

Asylum-seekers may also have their cases rejected without being processed through the above 'full' asylum procedures; their cases being rejected as 'clearly unfounded'. Usually, those rejected in such a law have very limited rights of appeal in the UK; the Nationality, Immigration and Asylum Act 2002 will further restrict the right of appeal in the UK of this group.

In addition to those who apply for asylum, the UK also hosts other populations of forced migrants. They include those who have arrived on 'programmes' – Government-sponsored evacuations such as the Vietnamese, Bosnian and Kosovan Programme. Here an immigration status is granted overseas and there is usually an organised reception programme. The Vietnamese were granted refugee status while Bosnians and Kosovars were only afforded temporary protection in the UK (the latter had one year's leave to remain). Other endangered people including Afghans, Iraqis and Zimbabweans, have secured entry to the UK on new Home Office migration programmes.

Other groups of forced migrants include those who fear persecution but never apply for asylum, relying on other immigration status or perhaps none at all. There are also migrations of refugees around Europe; movement into the UK made most significantly by Somalis who were originally granted refugee status in The Netherlands or Sweden. An estimated 9,000 Somalis have arrived from the EU.

Demography

In 2002 some 85,865 asylum applications were received in the UK (Home Office, 2002a). Including dependants, this amounted to 110,700 asylum-seekers who arrived in the UK in 2001. Most asylum applicants are single and male; less than 25 per cent of applicants have had dependent children in recent years, although the proportions of dependent children do vary among national groups.

The main countries of origin of asylum-seekers are listed in Table A1.1. During 2002, the four main countries of origin of asylum-seekers arriving in the UK were Iraq, Afghanistan, Zimbabwe and Somalia; countries beset by armed conflict, severe violations of human rights or both.

The Home Office publishes basic statistical data about asylum application and decisions, quarterly. The National Asylum Support Service, too, is meant to inform receiving health authorities and education authorities of asylum applicants dispersed to their area, but this system regularly breaks down. There is, therefore, little demographic data about the composition of asylum-seeking households or settlement patterns in the UK that would be of use to service providers, and Census data does not include information on immigration status (Castles *et al.*, 2001). The Home Office Research and Statistics Division is, however, planning to conduct demographic research on refugee settlement patterns in 2002/03.

An attempt to remedy this lack of data on refugee children has been made at the London Metropolitan University (GLA, 2002 forthcoming). By collecting local education authority (LEA) language and refugee surveys, Rutter concluded that there were about 80,000 asylum-seeking and refugee children in UK schools in January 2002. In Greater London schools and LEA nurseries there were an estimated 62,666 asylum-seeking and refugee children – their numbers comprised 6.04 per cent of the total pupil roll in Greater London (see Table A1.3). In seven London LEAs, refugee children comprise more than 10 per cent of the total school roll. Outside London, only Manchester and Glasgow LEAs have numbers of asylum-seeking and refugee children that approach that of London LEAs.

The largest groups of asylum-seeking and refugee children in schools are Somalis and Somali minority groups such as the Bravanese, comprising about 21 per cent of all asylum-seeking and refugee children in the UK. Sri Lankan Tamils are the next largest group and other large populations include Afghans, Turkish Kurds, Iranians and Congolese. In many LEAs, there is great national diversity among refugee communities – in one London LEA the refugee survey showed children coming from 58 national groups.

Asylum-seeking and refugee children are a very mobile population within the UK, owing to the temporary nature of housing allocated to asylum-seekers, and the fact that most refugees, once granted status, are then placed on a local authority waiting list for housing (Dobson *et al.*, 2000).

The analysis of data on asylum-seeking and refugee children, as well as of statistics produced by NASS (the National Asylum Support Service), indicate that secondary migration to Greater London is occurring. This is not a new phenomenon as there has been considerable secondary migration of other recent refugee groups to the capital (see, for example, Robinson and Hale, 1989). Push and pull factors in this secondary migration include existing community, family and friends, work and safety.

Language surveys and refugee data show two other important trends. First, asylum-seeking and refugee children are under-represented in LEA nursery schools and most classes of LEAs, and secondly, within an LEA, asylum-seeking and refugee children attend some schools and not others. This has implications for schools and LEAs and is discussed later.

Legislative changes and asylum-seeking children

There have been major changes in asylum legislation and policy since the late 1980s, with new laws passed in 1993, 1996, 1999 and 2002. Legislative changes have been accompanied by negative media coverage, particularly in tabloid and local newspapers. Arguably, the impact of such coverage makes it less likely that central and local government will invest in good support services for asylum-seekers and refugees. Public hostility to refugees is also increased by negative media coverage, and recent research cites over 50 per cent of refugee children reporting racist bullying (Richman, 1995; Save the Children, 1997).

The legislative and policy changes have:

- built 'barriers', making the legal entry of asylum-seekers much more difficult. Such barriers include the requirement of a visa to enter the UK and placing immigration officers at overseas airports

- restricted asylum-seekers' social and legal rights, including rights to work, benefits, housing and higher education

- tightened the substantive by which asylum cases are judged, so that proportionally more asylum-seekers are refused refugee status or ELR than in the late 1980s.

These legislative changes target the legal protection of asylum-seekers as well as welfare and social support systems for them. All legislation that affects asylum-seeking households will affect children's welfare. For example, proposals to remove some asylum-seekers' right to appeal in the UK against a negative asylum decision will obviously affect an adult asylum-seeker *and* his/her child dependants. There is an extensive literature, as well as much research about the asylum system and legal protection; these changes are not the primary focus of this report. However, the effects of these changes on young children's welfare is less well-documented; these issues are discussed in greater length in this report.

The legislative changes comprise the:

- Asylum and Immigration (Appeals) Act 1993

- Asylum and Immigration Act 1996

- Immigration and Asylum Act 1999

- Nationality, Immigration and Asylum Act 2002.

The Asylum and Immigration (Appeals) Act 1993

Among its many sections, this Act restricted rights to social housing for asylum-seekers. From its implementation, asylum-seekers lost the right to be accepted as homeless if they had any other housing, 'however temporary', in which they could live. Moreover, while an asylum case is being determined, no asylum-seeking household could be offered a secure social housing tenancy.

Schools, LEAs and organisations working with refugees noted increases in asylum-seeking children's mobility from the implementation of the Asylum and Immigration (Appeals) Act 1993 (see, for example, Power *et al.*, 1998; Dobson *et al.*, 2000; Rutter, 2001). Greater London OFSTED reports during the period 1993–1996 cited pupil mobility in some schools that had large numbers of asylum-seeking pupils as being 10 per cent in a year, and among the asylum-seeking pupils themselves as being 60–100 per cent (Rutter, 1999).

High pupil mobility among asylum-seeking and refugee pupils remains a major challenge today, particularly in Greater London. Pupil mobility and poor housing affect children's welfare and educational achievement. Ill-health, cramped play and study space, difficulties in securing school places, stigmatisation of homeless pupils and difficulties in building social relationships within the school are effects described by practitioners (Power *et al.*, 1998). Continuity of care for refugee children with healthcare or special educational needs is adversely affected. Other pupils, too, are affected by high pupil mobility: teacher time is spent settling in new students and it is difficult to deliver a curriculum with continuity in situations where there is high pupil mobility. There are therefore, social costs associated with high housing mobility.

Asylum and Immigration Act 1996

Further asylum legislation was passed in 1996, after the removal, in 1995, of Income Support from some asylum-seekers and then a reversal of this policy following legal challenges. The Asylum and Immigration Act 1996 had major effects on children's welfare. It barred asylum-seekers from being placed on a waiting list for social housing. It also removed the right to Income Support from asylum-seekers who lodged their claims 'in-country' as opposed to the port of entry. Families with children were instead supported by social services departments under the provisions of the Children Act 1989 and given a cash allowance and some form of temporary accommodation. Many such families were moved to temporary accommodation outside Greater London, often in seaside towns in locations such as Southend, Great Yarmouth, Bognor Regis and Hastings. Some of the accommodation used was of very poor quality. There were problems securing legal advice and service providers usually had little experience in working with asylum-seekers and little access to interpreters. Securing funding to work with new populations also proved a problem, as statutory funding sources such as the Ethnic Minority Achievement Grant rely on stable populations in the allocation of funding through formulae.

The duties placed on social services by the Asylum and Immigration Act 1996 may also have had long-term consequences on social services support to asylum-seeking and refugee families. This is described later.

Immigration and Asylum Act 1999

By 31 March 1999, Greater London social services departments were responsible for 20,421 asylum-seeking households without access to benefits and supported under the provisions of the Children Act 1989 and the National Assistance Act 1948 (London Research Centre, 1999). These local authorities were not being fully compensated by central government for support given to such asylum-seekers. After extensive lobbying from south-eastern local authorities, the Immigration and Asylum Act 1999 was passed and introduced far-reaching changes to the way that asylum-seekers were to be supported and housed in the UK. The Act set up the National Asylum Support Service (NASS) as part of the Immigration and Nationality Directorate of the Home Office. To prepare for dispersal, the UK was divided into regional groupings, termed 'asylum consortia'. Each consortium appointed officers to plan for services for asylum-seekers.

During Spring and Summer 2000, NASS introduced a new voucher and dispersal system for all new asylum-seekers in the UK, apart from unaccompanied asylum-seeking children. On arrival, any destitute asylum-seeker and dependants had the option of applying to NASS for a 'support only' package, or for support and accommodation. Until April 2002, support entailed a cash allowance of £10 per person per week, plus vouchers exchangeable at designated retail outlets. (NASS vouchers were abolished in April 2002 and replaced by a cash allowance. However, small numbers of asylum-seeking families may still be in receipt of vouchers from local authorities where they lodged their asylum claim 'in-country' between 1996 and 1999.)

NASS also allocates housing to those that apply for it. A mixture of public and private sector accommodation is used in regions of dispersal. Table A1.2 lists the areas of dispersal.

The NASS system has had a major effect on children's education and well-being, namely:

- Asylum-seekers may have a long wait in emergency accommodation in London prior to dispersal – far longer than the seven days planned by NASS. Most of the accommodation is in hotels previously or also used by homeless families. Some children living in emergency accommodation have stayed there so long that their parents have successfully got school places in London. Concerns about the quality of food in emergency accommodation for pregnant and nursing mothers has also been raised by healthcare practitioners and refugees themselves (McLeish, 2002).

- Inefficiencies in the processing of NASS vouchers. Those applying for support from NASS may wait many weeks before support is granted. A proportion of NASS vouchers are also lost in delivery. This places stress on already destitute families.

- Housing quality for those opting for NASS 'support only' and remaining with a host family and/or friends is an issue of concern; it is inevitably overcrowded and this will affect children's well-being and ability to study. This is a particular problem in Greater London where the latest available NASS figures show that 14,120 individuals have opted for support only (Home Office, 2002a). There is also an impact on the hosting household, whose living space and scarce household income is shared among more people.

- Housing mobility in London – anecdotal evidence from refugee support teachers is that many families who opt for 'support only' move between different types of accommodation, as hospitality is exhausted.

- Poverty: although voucher support was replaced by cash support on 8 April 2002, asylum-seekers are still supported at levels below income support. This is again of particular concern in Greater London, where those opting for 'support only' may be hosted by others on benefits. An account of the poverty faced by many asylum-seekers is provided in *Poverty and Asylum in the UK* where 85 per cent of a sample of refugee organisations reported that their clients experienced hunger on a regular basis (Refugee Council and Oxfam, 2002).

- School uniform, a requirement by most primary and secondary schools, is outside the budget of families supported by NASS. Yet school uniform grants are discretionary and some LEAs do not award them at all.

- Secondary migration to London, once the asylum applicant and dependants have been granted refugee status or ELR, is high.

- Parental stress: research on psychological risk factors in refugee children has concluded that one of the most important factors is the presence and quality of parenting (see for example, Ahearn and Athey, 1991; Richman, 1995). Any social policy intervention that places greater stress on refugee parents – isolation, stress or extreme poverty – will probably render a child less likely to cope.

The Nationality, Immigration and Asylum Act 2002

This will have far-reaching implications for young asylum-seeking children's welfare.

The parts of the Act that deal with asylum will again change the support arrangements for some asylum-seekers. From 2002, many newly arrived asylum-seekers will be held in non-secure 'Induction Centres' in London and the South East. Here they will lodge an asylum application, and, if needed, an application for support by NASS. After a period of time in the Induction Centre, the asylum-seeker may:

- go to a *removal centre* (detention centre) prior to removal from the UK. Two removal centres presently have facilities to detain children with their parents, prior to removal. Continued concerns have been expressed by children's charities about this detention of children, especially as accounts emerge of children being detained for substantial periods.

- move into the *community*, to live with family or friends, but be required to sign on at a reporting centre. Most asylum-seekers choosing this option are likely to be living in the Greater London area, with its large refugee population. At present, asylum-seekers who choose this option will continue to receive NASS support, but there is scope within the Bill for this to be removed at the Home Secretary's discretion. Refugee organisations believe that the eventual removal of this 'support only' option is likely.

- move to *dispersal accommodation* provided for NASS as before. At the time of writing, no extra money has been earmarked in order to make dispersal work and reduce secondary migration back to Greater London.

- move into an *accommodation centre*, where the asylum-seeker and his or her dependants will be expected to stay while their case is determined. The Home Office plans for the centres to be large, housing up to 750 residents. Food, other necessities, healthcare and education will be provided in these accommodation centres and the asylum-seeker will only receive a small amount of pocket money. All of the accommodation centres will be located outside the South East and there are plans to set up four pilots to be operational by 2004. The Home Office intends for 10,000 places per year to be provided in accommodation centres at a cost of £250 million over a three-year period, pending Treasury approval. (Some 30 per cent of all asylum-seekers could be housed in the centres). Home Office criteria for judging the success of the accommodation centres include reducing community tensions and illegal working. However, refugee agencies argue that the agenda behind accommodation centres is that of expediting speedy removal after an asylum claim is rejected.

The above changes are likely to affect children's welfare. Secondary migration to Greater London may remain at a high level if no extra funding is allocated to support arrangements in areas of dispersal. Housing in accommodation centres will increase isolation from the host community and prevent an asylum-seeker making local links outside Greater London. This, too, will encourage secondary migration to Greater London.

The proposal to provide separate education in accommodation centres for children has attracted particular criticism (see, for example, 'Asylum centre education "might breach human rights"', *Guardian*, 21 June 2002). Teacher unions, LEAs, head teachers, children's organisations and refugee agencies have campaigned vocally against this proposal, arguing that separate education is undesirable. Numerous studies have shown that, for refugee children, inclusion within mainstream education has special significance (see, for example, Rutter, 2001, pp. 92–3). Attending school may be a therapeutic and normalising experience for a child whose recent life experiences have been far from normal. Separate education has linguistic disadvantages – children have little or no social and academic interaction with native speakers of English – and asylum-seeking children are often successful ambassadors for their communities, therefore separate education will remove this aspect of community cohesion.

Separate education may prove difficult to deliver in accommodation centres. Unless the DfES sanctions disapplication, the accommodation centre contractors will be obliged to follow the National Curriculum. That there will be small numbers of school-aged children of very different ages in accommodation centres gives an indication of how difficult it will be to provide education.

The Nationality, Immigration and Asylum Act provides for other legislative changes that affect children. These are:

- A government resettlement programme for refugees admitted from abroad for resettlement in the UK, likely to be similar to the Vietnamese, Bosnian or Kosovan programmes. It is likely that such programmes will comprise a greater proportion of children than among 'spontaneous' arrivals.

- Sections that provide for the removal of the NASS 'support only' option if requested by the Home Secretary, or the removal of any NASS support. At present, significant numbers of asylum-seekers choose the existing 'support only' option, including many families with children. Most of this group remain within Greater London, near to existing communities. It seems likely that their removal of the support only option would not discourage many asylum-seekers from remaining in the capital. Instead it would only reduce their income, to the detriment of children's welfare. NASS support was withdrawn from in-country asylum applicants without dependent children in January 2003 (this move is presently being challenged in the courts). Although not directly targeting asylum-seeking children, it should be noted that many families from refugee communities – often with very few financial resources themselves – will feed and house destitute relatives and friends. There will be an indirect affect on children of families hosting destitute asylum-seekers as there was in 1996 after benefits were withdrawn from in-country applicants.

- Changes to the detention procedures, including removing the right to bail. Concurrently, the Home Office is commissioning increased places in removal centres, including places for families, and has publicly stated that the detention of children may be 'an unusual but necessary step' (Home Office, 2002b). This may be challenged legally: in a recent Legal Opinion, Nicholas Blake QC and barrister Sandhya Drew stated,

… there is an incompatibility with the Convention (on the Rights of the Child), where the detention of children who are seeking asylum is concerned… It is inconceivable that the best interests principle could contemplate even the short term detention of child asylum seekers for administrative convenience whilst their protection claims are processed. This applies irrespective of whether there are grounds to detain adult members of their families. Children are a vulnerable category and detention has a harsher impact on them than on adults.

In addition to changes in the present legislation, the Government is likely to change support systems for unaccompanied asylum-seeking and refugee children, most of whom are presently the responsibility of a small number of local authorities in Greater London and the South East, with Kent County Council alone being responsible for over 1,000 unaccompanied children, many of whom are moved to other parts of the UK. Options being debated are threefold. First, some four local authorities – Kent, West Sussex, Hillingdon and Croydon – would be responsible for assessing all unaccompanied children. Those children who needed homes would be dispersed around the UK. Finally, some of the case responsibility for these children would shift to the receiving local authority, an option that may require an amendment to the Children Act 1989.

Asylum-seekers lost the right to work in July 2002. This policy change may have indirect effects on asylum-seeking and refugee children. For example, asylum-seekers may choose to remain in London and other big metropolitan areas where their chances of finding undocumented work are higher.

Other non-asylum legislation and policy has affected asylum-seeking and refugee children, for example the introduction of school league tables made some schools less willing to admit pupils deemed to bring down results, including many newly arrived refugee children. These changes are discussed later in this report.

The next decade is likely to bring further legislative and policy changes affecting asylum-seeking children. At a European level, too, there is also likely to be greater harmonisation of the reception conditions of asylum-seekers with a draft directive on reception conditions, as well as their rights to welfare, housing, education and healthcare (European Commission, 2001). Although it is uncertain whether the draft directive will be passed, the trend is for greater harmonisation across Europe, and such changes will have a major impact on asylum-seeking children. Researchers engaged with refugee issues must be able to react to rapidly changing policies.

Refugee children's needs

Several researchers have attempted to develop profiles of refugee children's experiences and needs (see for example, Save the Children, 1997; Candappa, 2000). There is also an extensive psychological literature, which attempts to analyse refugee children's experiences and needs (see 'Gaps in knowledge' section). Such profiling is useful for service providers. It is important to remember that within a given refugee community there is a great deal of heterogeneity, but needs and problems that manifest themselves with significant numbers of refugee children include:

- having an interrupted education in the country of origin

- having horrific experiences in their home countries and during their flight to the UK (for a small number, this affects their ability to settle and rebuild their lives)

- living with families who experience a drop in their standard of living and status in society

- changing care arrangements: losing parents or usual carers

- having parents who are emotionally absent

- living with families who do not know their legal and social rights in the UK, including their rights to basic services such as education and healthcare, and who encounter problems securing education, healthcare or benefits

- speaking little or no English on arrival.

The need for legal protection and a secure immigration status in the UK is a universal need. To be treated as a child, first and foremost, rather than an asylum-seeker or refugee is a right that should underpin responses to these children.

Services

Asylum-seeking and refugee children are users of statutory services such as early years services, education, healthcare and social services. Such services, for example schooling, may be universal. Refugee children may also be users of targeted services, for refugees, for minority ethnic communities or for other identified vulnerable groups. These may be provided by statutory service providers – a refugee support team in education is one such example. Non-governmental organisations also run targeted support for refugee children.

Existing provision, concerns and unmet needs are described in the following chapters, collected from existing sources and supplemented by focus group discussions and visits.

2 Early years provision

Entitlements

Race relations legislation would indicate that asylum-seeking and refugee children have full entitlements to early years provision throughout the UK, although no government has issued any guidance on this.

Needs

Refugee communities have a great need for quality early years provision. The age profile of refugee communities in the UK is younger than the non-refugee population – in 1996 some 77 per cent of asylum applicants were under 35 years – and it is likely that there are proportionally more refugee children under five than in the population as a whole (Home Office, 1997). All research on employment among asylum-seekers and refugees indicates that the majority of these households are workless. Many refugee children grow up in poverty. Government commitments to abolish child poverty and to increase early years provision will, therefore, be of particular importance for refugee households.

Access to good quality early years provision is also likely to be a cost effective intervention. Children with positive early experiences of education are less likely to fail in school. Refugee Council research conducted in 1998 indicated that over 70 per cent of asylum-seeking and refugee children grew up in households where little or no English was spoken (Rutter and Hyder, 1998). Enabling a child from a non-English speaking household to attend a nursery before school starts will decrease the need for funded support in primary school. Access to early years provision may also enable refugee parents to attend English classes or obtain new qualifications. And for the most stressed refugee parents, a break from the demands of childcare may enable them to rebuild their lives, saving later interventions by health and social care agencies.

Present provision

Central government initiatives

There has been an expansion of early years provision during the last five years, a policy central to government targets to reduce child poverty.

In England, initiatives of potential relevance to refugee families include:

- *The Neighbourhood Childcare Initiative.* This is an area-based initiative that aims to create 45,000 new daycare places in up to 900 neighbourhood nurseries (mostly voluntary sector), together with 25,000 new places at child minders. The aim of this initiative is to improve access to childcare for working parents living in the most deprived areas (Daycare Trust, 2002)

- *Sure Start.* This is an area-based initiative that aims to ensure that every child arrives in school healthy and ready to learn. It funds a range of projects including parent and toddler groups, advice sessions and provision in family centres. In Greater London a small number of Sure Start programmes have worked with refugee families, with some, such as Sure Start Edmonton, targeting these families. By March 2004 it is intended that 500 Sure Start projects will be working with 400,000 of the most deprived children.

- *The Four-Year-Old Grant and the Three-Year-Old Grant.* All four year olds whose parents want to use nursery care are now guaranteed such provision – up to five two-and-a-half hour sessions during term time, achieved by payment of a grant to nurseries.

- *Early Excellence Centres.* These provide a range of early years education and family support services on one site, building on the pioneering work of the Dorothy Gardner centre in Westminster and others. Such centres provide nursery education, and services such as health visitor clinics, family literacy and English language classes, toy libraries, and surgeries offering welfare rights and other advice and services. It is intended that the funding for the 29 pilot Early Excellence Centres be expanded to fund some 100 such centres by 2004. Given the multiple social needs of many refugee families, Early Excellence Centres may usefully meet their needs and many are doing so already.

In 1999, the new English Early Years Development Plans were required to account for services provided for refugee children; an addition welcomed by refugee charities. Local authority social service departments are also required by the Department of Health to draw up Children's Services Plans – a product of collaboration between local authorities, health authorities, the voluntary sector and other appropriate groups. This creates another opportunity for planning for the needs of young refugee children. OFSTED is required to inspect all nurseries and other childcare, including child minders, and these inspections require an assessment of whether children's ethnic or linguistic needs are being met.

Despite these and other central government initiatives, such as a commitment to better training for early years workers, it is likely that many refugee families are not reaping the full benefits of expanded early years provision. There is also no evidence to indicate that refugee communities groups are being helped to develop their own nurseries, parent and toddler groups or other provision. The reasons are complex, but mostly relate to a lack of bridge-building between early years partnerships and refugee community groups. They are discussed below.

Regional initiatives

None of the asylum consortia has examined early years issues.

Local authorities and individual institutions

Here there is growing consensus as to what makes good early years provision, although there are wide variations in practice. Good practice comprises many of the following:

- Having a person with designated responsibility for refugees located within an early years team/partnership at LEA level.

- Effective multi-agency work, in particular ensuring that there are good links between health visitors and early years educators. Focus group discussion and visits indicated that such linking was weak in many areas.

- Conducting detailed ethnic monitoring of uptake of early years services.

- Child minding, which offers employment opportunities to refugee women. Local authorities can organise training courses targeted at refugee women, perhaps with English language support. Training should be coupled with a small grants scheme to enable the women to purchase toys and safety equipment.

- Ensuring availability of good quality outreach and consultation to gather information on needs and to inform refugee parents of the range of early years provision.

- Helping refugee community organisations to develop their own early years services, for example parent and toddler groups. Within Greater London, only five refugee community organisations presently run such services.

- Training early years workers to enable them to better meet the needs of refugee children. Refugee children need nurseries and playgroups that can:
  - meet their psychological needs by, for example, using play to help a child settle
  - respond to their language needs
  - challenge racism and promote cultural diversity
  - involve parents who may not be confident in speaking English
  - support families who may be experiencing stress and economic deprivation. (A more detailed description of good practice is given in Rutter and Hyder, 1998; Save the Children/Refugee Council, 2001; Rutter, 2001.)

Concerns

Access to early years provision

Despite growing consensus about good practice there are concerns about early years provision for refugee children. All available research indicates that refugee children presently have unequal access to early years provision. For example, research conducted by the author in 1998 and 2002, and by the London Borough of Islington Women's Equality Unit, indicates that refugee children are under-represented in most forms of early years provision (GLA, 2002 forthcoming; Rutter and Hyder, 1998). However, the analysis of language and refugee surveys conducted in 2002 does indicate an improvement in refugee children's access to LEA nurseries in some London LEAs since 1998, including three that had attempted to conduct outreach work among refugee communities. However, despite an expansion of early years provision, inequality persists. In one London local authority, where refugee children comprise 6.5 per cent of all children, there were only nine refugee children within the area's nursery provision in 1997. Reasons for under-representation include:

- *Housing mobility:* many LEA nurseries have waiting lists for places, and families move before a nursery place is available.

- *Lack of knowledge of local services:* many refugee-producing countries in Africa and Asia have little or no early years provision. Asylum-seeking families arriving in the UK seldom know about the range of early years provision available. And since over 70 per cent of asylum-seekers speak little or no English, it is difficult for parents to find out about provision. In particular, they may not know about projects such as parent and toddler groups, one o'clock clubs, play buses and toy libraries.

- *Lack of outreach by early years providers/partnerships.*

- *Poverty:* even parent and toddler groups that only make a small charge might be unaffordable for an asylum-seeking family that is forced to live on NASS support.

- *Cultural factors:* in some refugee communities infants are always cared for by the mother and her extended family, so putting them in the care of strangers could attract disapproval. Other mothers, particularly those who speak little English, feel uneasy about young children being cared for by people who do not know their language, dietary arrangements, religion or customs.

- *Inaccessibility:* some early years provision may not be accessible for large families without private transport.

- *Unwelcoming services:* some types of early years provision, such as playgroups and one o'clock clubs, may be used by a regular group of children and carers who may make 'outsiders' feel unwelcome.

Poor quality ethnic monitoring

This was an issue that was mentioned in all visits and focus group research conducted by the author. It was felt that most early years providers did not undertake good quality ethnic monitoring that would highlight differences in the uptake of early years services among refugee communities. Additionally refugee community groups felt that Early Years Development Partnerships and LEAs did not have accurate demographic information about the local population and this was a barrier to extending services for refugees and targeting resources.

Lack of evaluation

There is little evaluation of service provision that takes into account refugee children's particular needs. Given that in some London local authorities, refugee children account for more than 10 per cent of all children, and a greater proportion of those living in low-income households, it would be reasonable to expect Sure Start evaluations to analyse its applicability to refugee children.

Area-based targeting

Sure Start and the Neighbourhood Childcare Initiative are targeted at deprived families living in particular areas. Refugee children (and others) living in temporary accommodation in the more prosperous areas can be missed by area-based programmes.

3 Education

Legal entitlements

Asylum-seeking children, as well as those with ELR and Refugee Status have full entitlement to compulsory education throughout the UK. In England, the entitlement of asylum-seekers and refugees to compulsory education between 5 and 16 years is outlined in the DfES Code of Practice on School Admissions, Annex B, giving them the same rights to education as other children. Section 14 of the Education Act 1996 also obliges English LEAs to provide a full-time education to all children resident within the LEA. In Wales, the Code of Practice on Admissions 1999 secures the right to education for asylum-seeking and refugee children, and in Scotland their entitlement to education is premised on the Education (Scotland) Act 1980.

Other legislation and guidance of particular relevance for asylum-seeking and refugee children in education includes:

- A legal right for free school meals if that family is in receipt of a means tested benefit (Education Act 1996) or being supported by NASS or a local authority under the interim support scheme (Section 73 and 117, Schedule 14, Immigration and Asylum Act 1999).

- English LEAs have a duty to provide certain educational support to children who are 'looked after' under Section 20 of the Children Act 1989, as are many unaccompanied refugee children under the age of 16 years. This duty requires the LEA to provide an officer who has responsibility for the education of 'looked after' children and an individual education plan and ensures that a child who has newly come into care is not out of education for more than 20 days.

- English and Welsh LEAs and schools must comply with the Race Relations Act 1976 and the Race Relations (Amendment) Act 2000. The latter obliges LEAs and other public bodies to positively promote good race relations. Additionally, the Commission for Racial Equality is tasked under the 2000 Act to prepare a statutory Code of Practice for LEAs and schools on how to fulfil their race equality duties. The new Education Code of Practice came into force in 2002.

- In England, OFSTED can inspect schools for social inclusion, including support for refugee children (OFSTED, 2000).

Present provision

Central government

The DfES maintains a small team whose brief includes traveller education, refugee education and intercultural education. The team is located in the School Inclusion Division and has recently published guidance on the education of asylum-seeking and refugee children (DfES, 2002). OFSTED also employs three inspectors whose brief includes refugees. The Scottish Executive and the Welsh Assembly have members of staff whose brief includes refugee children's education, but neither has issued guidance about the education of refugee children.

Central government's role includes the planning and implementation of targeted funding initiatives. In England, three particular interventions are of particular relevance to young refugee children: the Ethnic Minority Achievement Grant (EMAG), the Vulnerable Children Fund and the Children's Fund.

EMAG is part of the School Standards Fund and replaced the Home Office Section 11 Fund. The DfES provides 57 per cent of the grant, with local government being responsible for the remainder. EMAG is used mostly to fund English as an additional language support, although it also funds many refugee support teachers. The operation of the EMAG fund has attracted criticism and it is widely felt not to meet the needs of refugee children because:

- Funding is insufficient to meet refugee children's real needs. In reality, teachers' time is solely targeted at beginners in English. Few children who have achieved some competence in English receive additional help and EMAG does not meet the needs of children whose needs are more complex.

- Funding has decreased at a time when the number of children needing support has increased. A Section 11 fund of £130.8 million in 1993/94 was cut to an EMAG fund of £83 million in 1998/99.

- There is no contingency in the EMAG grant. Local authorities have to make an annual bid for EMAG funds, yet the arrival of asylum-seeking children in a local authority is usually unpredictable, with many LEAs unable to claim monies for children who arrive mid-way through a financial year. As asylum-seekers began to be dispersed outside London, many coastal and northern local authorities complained that they were not receiving additional monies to meet the students' needs.

- EMAG is reluctant to allocate grants for funding dedicated educational psychologists and educational social workers to support refugee children. But good practice indicates that the complex needs of refugee children are best met by multi-disciplinary teams.

- EMAG does not fund home language teaching, even though this has educational and psychosocial benefits for refugee children. The DfES policy is that home language teaching is the responsibility of communities.

In response to the above criticisms of EMAG, the DfES introduced the new Vulnerable Children Fund in late 2002. This new fund can be used to support travellers, asylum-seeking children and other children out of school. In 2003 its total budget will comprise £84 million. Spending on specific groups is not laid down by the DfES, although in bidding for its monies the LEA has to show how the bid is linked to the Education Development Plan. Unlike EMAG, its monies do not have to be devolved to schools. It could be used to fund items such as dedicated educational psychologists to work with refugee children. It is a welcome development. However, the allocation of the Vulnerable Children Fund is based on an annual bid. There is no contingency. In 2002, the DfES rejected a contingency fund for large groups of asylum-seekers who arrive in an LEA or school outside deadlines for bidding for funds.

The DfES-administered Children's Fund has the potential to fund non-governmental organisations working with refugee communities, as well as welfare support. It is also meant to encourage inter-agency partnership. One London LEA has successfully channelled £330,000 of its Children's Fund to refugee projects. However, in other local authorities, refugee agencies as well as statutory service providers have complained that the Children's Fund has not been targeted at refugee communities.

In Wales, the Welsh Assembly makes grants available to local authorities for the support of children from ethnic minority communities. In Scotland there is no dedicated fund for such children's educational support, but funding is met directly by local authorities. There is no EMAG-like grant, as local authorities and the Scottish Executive argue that the needs of ethnic minority communities in Scotland can best be met by the appropriate delivery of mainstream local authority services.

Regional government

The regional asylum consortia employ officers whose responsibility includes planning for the arrival of asylum-seeking children (see Table A1.2). In some, although not all consortia, there are coordinating meetings of education officers held under the auspices of the consortia. However, to date there has been little impact on actual educational practice (and also other services for children) and no consortia have facilitated cross-LEA services.

Regional and inter-LEA cooperation is more complicated in London – where at least 70 per cent of asylum-seeking children are resident. Here LEAs are small and many organisations, including OFSTED and the Audit Commission, have argued for greater cooperation (OFSTED/Audit Commission, 2001). The London Asylum Seekers' Consortium (LASC) has not engaged in strategic planning. The Greater London Authority has produced a strategy report on asylum-seekers and refugees (as well as other relevant areas such as a children's strategy) but its remit does not extend to education or social services (GLA, 2001). The Government Office for London and the Association of London Government have had minimal involvement in refugee children's education in recent years.

Local government

During the last ten years there has been a growing consensus about good practice for refugee children at both LEA and school level (see for example Arshad *et al.*, 1999; Mott, 2000; Refugee Council, 2000; Rutter, 2001, pp. 74–83). This consensus has developed with little intervention from central government; indeed, many aspects of present DfES policy are inimical to the successful educational integration of refugee children. At LEA level, good practice for refugee children is likely to include:

- multi-agency planning at a local authority level, involving education, housing, other statutory services such as FE colleges, the police and the health service, as well as non-governmental organisations

- ensuring that the Education Development Plan (EDP) and its Welsh and Scottish equivalents targets refugee children and involves schools, as well as community stakeholders in drafting

- access to good quality interpreting and translation services

- ethnic monitoring, including monitoring of the uptake of non-compulsory educational services such as early years and youth work provision, as well as educational achievement and school exclusions

- LEA admissions practices that facilitate the early admission of refugee children to school

- the active involvement of educational psychology teams in assessment of refugee children, therapeutic work with them, advice for teachers and other professionals as well as in-service training for teachers

- the employment of refugee support teachers/teams (this appears to be important and is discussed below)

- programmes to support refugee community schools. About 40 per cent of all refugee children in the UK attend refugee community schools that may teach the home language, as well as supplementing the mainstream curriculum. A number of London LEAs fund and support such schools

- work by the youth service to ensure that refugee children have full access to youth clubs, leisure, mentoring, after-school and holiday projects and that refugee community organisations are supported in their development of youth services

- the active involvement of early years providers for services for refugee children (see above)

- work by libraries and leisure services to meet the particular needs of refuge communities, for example ensuring that refugees have access to books in their home languages. (Taken from Camden Education, 1996; Rutter and Hyder, 1998; Mott, 2000; Rutter, 2001 *inter alia.*)

In January 2002 some 34 local education authorities (LEAs) in England, Scotland and Wales employed specialist refugee support teachers or teams. A further two London LEAs have specialist refugee support teachers working with under fives. Job descriptions and working practices differ between LEAs, but refugee support teachers may:

- admit and settle asylum-seeking and refugee children into school before handing over responsibility for their education to mainstream and LEA teachers

- provide a total package of support, including English language support for refugee children

- support refugee children whose needs go beyond that of learning English, for example a child who is not coping as a result of an overwhelmingly traumatic past

- act as a contact point within the local authority and represent education on multi-agency working parties

- act in an advisory capacity – organising in-service training and helping schools develop practices.

A small number of LEAs have multi-disciplinary teams located in education whereby teachers work alongside social workers and/or psychologists. One London LEA employed such a team from 1993–1998 comprising a coordinator, six refugee support teachers, a family support worker and a part-time educational psychologist. It appeared to be an effective way of working with refugee children and their carers. However the team was disbanded in 1998 after changes in educational funding.

The employment of refugee support teachers appears to be particularly important in achieving good multi-agency coordination at LEA level. Without specialist refugee support teachers, there is often less planning and support for refugee children.

Other LEA staff may have designated responsibility for refugee children. These include bilingual classroom assistants working with specific refugee communities or linguistic groups, traveller educators, 'looked after children' educators and educational psychologists. Bilingual classroom assistants can offer real support to schools working with refugee children. As well as their linguistic skills, a good bilingual classroom assistant can promote liaison between home and school. For refugees, employment as a bilingual classroom assistant can also be the first step to achieving qualified teacher status in the UK. However, it should be noted that many bilingual classroom assistants have poor conditions of employment, earning less than £6 per hour and paid per session. Among London LEAs, only Somali-speaking bilingual classroom assistants are employed in significant numbers. It has been particularly difficult to recruit and retain Persian-, Pushto- and Albanian-speaking classroom assistants in some parts of London. There is no research about bilingual classroom assistants who are refugees.

Schools

Here there is also growing consensus about good practice for refugee children at school level, comprising much of the following:

- policies that draw on past experiences of working with bilingual children, promoting anti-racist and multi-cultural education and working with children in temporary accommodation

- an identified member of staff in the school who has responsibility for refugee children and access to information about refugee children

- in-service training on meeting the needs of refugee children

- an examination of school admission and induction practices, to ensure that refugee children are made to feel welcome

- specialist help and strategies for refugee children who are not coping as a result of their past and present experiences

- adequate support for children with English as an additional language

- encouragement to maintain and develop the home language(s)

- action to counter hostility and the racist bullying of refugees. This may comprise links with other organisations such as Race Equality Councils and community groups. School also need effective sanctions against racist bullying and to use the curriculum to promote ethnic diversity as positive

- good home–school liaison

(Source: Refugee Council, 2000).

Concerns

Despite a growing consensus on what constitutes good education and quality provision for refugee children, there are continuing concerns about refugee children's education. These concerns, described below, have been articulated by refugees themselves, teachers and other educationalists (see for example Save the Children, 1997; Mott, 2000; Rutter, 2001)

Access to schooling

Some asylum-seeking and refugee children face major barriers in securing school places (Community Health South London NHS Trust, 2001; Refugee Council, 2002). In July 2001, the Refugee Council estimated that there were at least 2,100 asylum-seeking and refugee children out of school in Greater London alone. There is anecdotal evidence that the situation has worsened since then, with the Children's Society estimating in October 2001 that there were at least 700 asylum-seeking and refugee children out of school in the London Borough of Newham alone (*Guardian Education*, 13 January 2002). Failure to secure a school place has multiple causes, including:

1   an acute shortage of school places in some LEAs and these LEAs being unwilling or unable to fulfil their statutory duty to provide a school place

2   an unwillingness by some schools to admit refugee pupils. Although pupils with English language needs who arrive in English schools in Years 5, 6, 10 or 11 of their schooling no longer have to be included in English school or LEA league tables, the unwillingness to admit some refugee pupils has persisted. This is most acute for those children who arrive in the UK aged 14–16, during an examination course, as many schools feel that they have little to offer such pupils

3   high housing mobility among asylum-seeking and refugee pupils, making for frequent moves of school

4   asylum-seeking and refugee parents being unaware of their rights to a school place and having no access to legal representation and/or advocacy to help them secure compulsory education

5   confusing school admissions procedures which differ greatly between LEAs and schools. Many refugee parents are also unaware that a place on a school waiting list will not usually mean that a school place is allocated

6   failure to access school uniform and travel grants acting as a barrier to securing a school place.

Unequal access to some schools within an LEA

Within LEAs, asylum-seeking and refugee children are not evenly distributed among schools (an issue more marked at secondary school level). Those refugee children who arrive in the UK outside the normal school admission cycle will only secure places in schools with spaces; schools that are often less popular with more settled groups of parents. In many cases these are schools that face long-standing challenges and problems.

Demographic analysis undertaken at London Metropolitan University indicates that refugee children are also less likely to secure places in Roman Catholic and Church of England schools. Many refugee families from Europe, Latin America, west and central Africa are observant Christians; lack of access to church schools is an issue that must be monitored.

Underachievement among some groups of refugee pupils

There is growing evidence to show that some groups of asylum-seeking and refugee children are underachieving in schools. These groups include Somalis, Turkish Kurdish boys and eastern European Roma (see, for examples, Ali and Jones, 2000; Rutter, 2003). However, LEA data about refugee pupil achievement are variable in quality as, in many LEAs, ethnic categories (Black African, Black other etc.) used in data analysis are too broad to highlight underachievement (and success) among particular refugee groups.

The reasons for such underachievement is likely to be multi-factoral and complex and there is a need for national research on this, as well as better data collection on school achievement.

Bullying and racial harassment

This is another concern articulated by refugee children. For example, of 32 children, many of primary school age, interviewed in Hackney in 1996, 19 report being the victim of racial harassment and seven had moved school as a result (Richman, as cited in Rutter, 2001). Children reported verbal abuse, theft of personal items, spitting and physical attack. Given that the Race Relations (Amendment) Act obliges schools and LEAs to promote good race relations, there is room for research that monitors the effectiveness of such policies.

Special educational needs provision

There is no research that analyses refugee children's experiences of the special needs system – a clear gap in knowledge. In 2003, research was conducted in one London local authority about Congolese children. This research was commissioned after statistical analysis showed that 74 per cent of Congolese children had special educational needs, compared with 22 per cent of all children in that LEA (Rutter, 2003). However, in four case study schools (secondary) examined by the author, it was found that refugee children were under-represented among those children on the stages of the SEN Code of Practice. No comparable studies have been done in primary schools. While it might be expected that more refugee children would be classed as having special needs, three factors may prevent this:

1   poor communication with parents about a children's experiences in the home country

2   high housing mobility preventing continuity of care

3   the assumption held by many teachers that a newly arrived child's learning needs
mostly comprise the need to learn English. This may prevent some children with
specific or general learning difficulties receiving early support.

Among refugee children experiencing emotional and behavioural difficulties, support
is judged to be very patchy. There is a tendency for many such children resident in
London to be referred to the Medical Foundation for the Care of Victims of Torture,
whether the emotional and behavioural problems relate to the refugee experience or
not. A small number of educational psychology teams have developed experience in
assessing and supporting refugee children, as have a small number of Child and
Adolescent Mental Health Services. One educational psychology team (the London
Borough of Enfield) operates a system whereby a part-time educational psychologist
is attached to an education-based home–school liaison team for minority ethnic
children under five. The educational psychologist is involved in the assessment of
refugee children. She also undertakes some therapeutic work. Her job also involves
training and supporting early years workers and running a drop-in group for parents,
carers and professionals who have concerns about a particular child. This model of
working is judged to be cost effective and innovative and perhaps could be
replicated.

Educational funding

That the education funding system in both England and Wales does not meet the
needs of refugee children is of growing concern and may contribute to school and
LEA unwillingness to accept refugee children. Mainstream funding relies on an
annual pupil census and geographically mobile children who arrive and leave
between census dates attract no funding. There is a time-lag between a child arriving
and funding being granted, as well as lack of contingency funds, either in
mainstream funding or project funds such as the EMAG, available to local authorities
and schools to support significant numbers of unexpected arrivals. (See Rutter and
Stanton, 2001 and GLA, 2002, forthcoming, for a fuller discussion of funding.)

Youth work, holiday projects and after-school provision

Recent research has identified many gaps in youth work provision for refugee
children. *Out of Exile* surveyed present youth work provision for young refugees
(Norton and Cohen, 2000). Almost all of this was offered by the voluntary sector and
very little by local authorities. Refugee children also did not appear to be using much

non-targeted local authority youth work provision. Although youth work is an issue pertinent to older refugee children to a much greater extent, there does need to be increased partnership between local authority youth work teams and refugee organisations.

Another gap in provision is found in holiday projects that include English language support. An all too common scenario is of a refugee child who arrives in the UK in May or June, enrols at school and begins to learn until the summer holidays intervene. During this long vacation, many newly arrived English language learners lose their existing English language skills.

4 Healthcare

Asylum-seekers, as well as those with ELR and refugee status, have full entitlements to most health services throughout the UK. Asylum-seeking children supported by NASS, however, have no right to supplies of formula milk granted to other families receiving means tested benefits. While many of the healthcare needs of refugee children are similar to non-refugees, asylum-seeking and refugee children do have specific healthcare needs. These can be summarised as:

- securing access to healthcare

- issues around language and communication

- health issues relating to refugees' cultural or ethnic origin, for example, female genital mutilation, sickle-cell disease/trait and beta thallasaemia

- health issues relating to refugees' arrival from poorer countries that have weaker primary healthcare systems and where certain communicable diseases may be endemic, or where immunisation may not take place

- health issues caused by refugees' exposure to violence and persecution

- health issues relating to welfare in the UK, in particular nutrition.

Access to healthcare

Asylum-seekers and refugees have the same basic entitlement to healthcare as other UK residents, with this entitlement being outlined in Health Circular (82) 15. However, many asylum-seeking families, as well as unaccompanied children, experience extreme difficulty in securing access to healthcare. The reasons for this are complex. Newly arrived asylum-seekers may not know how the British healthcare system works and that GP registration provides the route to accessing healthcare. Refugees may also not know the range of services available to them, for example the work of health visitors. Lack of fluency in English may prevent a refugee accessing services.

Asylum-seekers and refugees may be refused registration with a GP; research conducted in east London in 2002 indicated that 34 per cent of a sample of 116 children were not registered with a GP (Refugee Council, 2002). Even if registered, many asylum-seekers face bureaucratic hurdles in securing healthcare. In order for asylum-seekers supported by NASS or local authorities to secure free prescriptions and dental care, they have to complete Dept of Health Form HC1, return it to a central NHS administration unit in order to be issued with HC2, a certificate of entitlement. The latter provides access to free prescriptions for six months, then the process has to be repeated. The fact that asylum-seekers and refugees are a very mobile population, particularly in Greater London, can also affect continuity of care.

Language and communication

Communication difficulties may prevent refugees from securing healthcare and also delay diagnosis. Face-to-face interpreters can be booked for planned appointments in most parts of London and other big cities, although they are often not available for appropriate languages outside big cities. There are telephone interpreting services that can be used, however using interpreters effectively is a task that requires skill and experience. Not all medical professionals possess this skill, particularly when examining children; this is an issue that could be remedied by more effective training.

Female genital mutilation

Despite being illegal in the UK since the passage of the Prohibition of Female Circumcision Act 1985, this is still a major health concern facing some refugee communities in the UK. Girls generally undergo this practice at a young age: between six and eight years is common. It is a controversial issue, generating strong feelings among refugees and healthcare professionals.

Female genital mutilation is practised in many African countries, as well as in Yemen and Oman, and in their refugee and migrant diaspora. It is carried out by Muslims, Christians, Jews and animists. Many people believe it is justified by religious teaching, although it has no basis in any religious creed. In some countries, female genital mutilation is part of a girl's rites of passage into adulthood. In some societies, too, an uncircumcised woman is viewed as shameful and unclean. The practice is also used by families as a means of controlling girls' sexuality, and to deter them from marrying outside their ethnic group.

Female genital mutilation takes three forms: circumcision, excision and infibulation. Circumcision involves cutting the hood of the clitoris, whilst excision involves the removal of the clitoris and all or part of the labia minora. The most severe form of genital mutilation is infibulation, which involves the removal of the clitoris, labia minora and part or all of the labia majora. The two sides of the vulva are then stitched together and eventually scar tissue forms. A small opening is left for the passage of urine and blood.

In the UK, female genital mutilation is an issue which mostly affects the Somali, Sudanese and Yemeni communities. Although illegal, the operation still takes place in the UK, amid great secrecy. Other parents take their daughters to Africa or the Middle East during the summer vacation. There are immediate risks to a girl's health, as well as long-term complications. An infibulated woman may suffer from chronic bladder and uterine infections. Sexual intercourse is likely to be painful for an infibulated woman. Complications during childbirth are unavoidable: in Somalia, a pregnant woman has her scar cut open and is then re-infibulated at every delivery. Labour is longer, and there is an increased risk of infection, maternal and child death and perinatal brain damage.

Those working with young refugee girls need to be aware of the practice and its consequences. Girls who have been infibulated are extremely unwilling to take part in physical education. They may frequently be absent, as menstruation can be very painful. It will also take an infibulated girl a very long time to pass urine: in schools where children have little privacy this can lead to questions, teasing and desperate embarrassment.

In both African and European countries there are promising initiatives among women's groups and from governments, aimed at ending the practice of female genital mutilation. Legislation in the UK prohibiting female genital mutilation came into force in 1985, with the Prohibition of Female Circumcision Act. Female genital mutilation has been incorporated into child protection legislation by local authorities, and there have been nearly 40 cases where there has been action to protect girls at risk. But intervention is often difficult, and many social workers face the dilemma of whether intervention will permanently divide a girl from her family. FORWARD, the Sudanese Women's Group and the London Black Women's Health Action Group are among the organisations working to eradicate the practice. Among the Somali and Sudanese communities, more and more individuals and organisations are willing to speak out against the practice, often in the face of hostility. They view female genital mutilation as a form of child abuse and an infringement of human rights, but educational campaigns among communities that practice female genital mutilation are underfunded, badly coordinated and do not reach all members of relevant communities (Dorkenoo and Ellworthy, 1994; Royal College of Paediatricians, 1999; Rutter, 2001).

Communicable diseases

There are a number of useful summaries of communicable diseases common among refugee populations (see Royal College of Paediatricians, 1999; Burnett and Fassil, 2002; harpweb). These infections vary according to the countries from which refugees have fled. Particular conditions to be aware of include gastrointestinal infections, parasites, tuberculosis and malaria. However, diagnosis of these conditions is often delayed in the UK (Royal College of Paediatricians, 1999). That primary healthcare breaks down in conditions of conflict also means that refugee children may not have received routine immunisations.

Responding to HIV/AIDS among refugee children requires national planning. In much of sub-Saharan Africa (and increasingly in parts of Russia and the Ukraine) the rate of HIV infection is high. In the Democratic Republic of Congo and Zimbabwe, both major refugee-producing countries, the ante-natal prevalence of HIV is so high that between 10–20 per cent of all children born have been vertically infected with HIV. Great stigma is attached to HIV infection and among many asylum-seekers there is the fear that HIV/AIDS will prevent an award of refugee status or ELR, and therefore treatment is often delayed. A recent court case granted formula milk to an HIV positive mother who was being supported by NASS, but the judgement only related to this woman. There have been other cases where HIV positive mothers have not been able to access formula milk. While excellent treatment, advice and support is available from the NHS and community groups, these services are mostly located in London and Manchester.

Psychosocial issues

There has been little research conducted in the UK about the psychological profiles and responses of refugee children (nor about effective psychological interventions). There is undoubtedly a significant number of refugee children whose life experiences manifest themselves in psychological distress. Some are supported in the school SEN system, and many are referred to the Medical Foundation. A small number come to the attention of Child and Adolescent Mental Health Services.

Nutrition

There is a growing body of research about nutritional status of refugee children – malnutrition among refugee children is not as uncommon as might be expected in a wealthy country. Those asylum-seekers who have spent time in refugee camps (Somalis in east Africa, for example) may suffer from malnutrition, as might those asylum-seekers who have had lengthy land journeys through many countries. Asylum-seekers and refugee children living in bed and breakfast hostels or in NASS emergency accommodation are also vulnerable. Hotels may lack cooking and hygienic food storage facilities; cooked food that is provided in emergency accommodation is not always acceptable to children. A research project has also raised concerns about infant nutrition among asylum-seeking families (McLeish, 2002). In emergency accommodation and NASS full board accommodation, formula milk is not provided – even where a mother is HIV positive. Neither is appropriate weaning and infant food usually provided. NASS-supported women are also not provided with formula milk tokens, although this is being legally challenged by the Child Poverty Action Group, acting on behalf of an HIV positive woman.

It is debatable whether asylum-seekers, supported by NASS at levels below Income Support, can achieve a balanced diet. Concerns have also been raised about the nutritional contribution of free school meals. Research carried out among Ugandan Asian children showed significant iron and protein malnutrition (Community Relations Commission, 1976). This was attributed to children wasting free school meals because the foodstuffs were largely unfamiliar or did not conform to religious requirements. While schools in urban areas have addressed this issue and now provide halal meals, it is likely that some refugee children are still nutritionally vulnerable.

More optimistically, research undertaken in 2000 on refugees' nutritional status showed that some groups of refugees may have better nutrition than other low income families (Sellen *et al.*, 2000). Refugee women's family feeding strategies were examined (most of the women were well-educated and were in contact with community groups). These women provided a balanced diet for their families, despite being supported by local authority vouchers under the provisions of the Children Act. They achieved this by sharing shopping and cooking. The maintenance of breastfeeding was also high, as a result of support systems among the women. The research shows some of the risks that isolated refugee families may face and the important role of community support.

Responses

As in education, a number of projects have been set up to improve refugees' access to and experiences of healthcare. The Department of Health has policy staff with responsibility for refugee healthcare and is in the process of developing national guidance on healthcare. Awareness of healthcare issues is improving and a new internet-based healthcare information exchange – harpweb – is serviced by the University of East London. Some of the asylum consortia have health working groups, mirroring provision in education.

A number of health authorities have funded direct work with refugees. Such responses include salaried GPs working with asylum-seekers living in hostels. The

South East London Health Authority employs a team whose responsibility includes the homeless and refugees. It was responsible for planning a Health Action Zones-funded project working in Lambeth, Southwark and Lewisham with refugee children. Some six staff are employed working with unaccompanied children, providing training for healthcare, educational and social care staff and improving planning and coordination in south London.

A number of primary care trusts employ health visitors with responsibility for homeless and refugee families. Additionally, some primary care trusts have salaried bilingual health advocates working with particular groups of refugees.

Education providers commission the school medical service. One school medical service has altered its tenders to ensure that homeless and refugee families always receive a medical examination on entry to school.

Non-governmental organisations also provide health advice and support. There are a growing number of healthcare projects working with refugee children – for example the Medical Foundation, described below. Barnardo's Positive Options provides support for children and families affected by HIV/AIDS, as do a number of London-based community groups such as the Ugandan Community Relief Association. However, outside Greater London there is very little support for asylum-seeking and refugee children affected by HIV/AIDS.

Concerns

Five concerns are widely articulated:

1   As described above, access to healthcare provides a major challenge for some asylum-seeking and refugee families.

2   Awareness of particular healthcare issues facing refugee children was also felt to be an issue, although all those interviewed felt that the level of awareness had improved in the last five years. Providing training and information among a fragmented service such as healthcare is also more challenging than among educational providers.

3   All those interviewed felt that health visitors and the school medical service had an essential role to play in ensuring access to healthcare and the support of mobile families. Although there is some excellent practice it was felt that the school medical service could be deployed more effectively.

4   Healthcare provision, particularly support for children manifesting emotional and behavioural problems, and paediatric HIV support was felt to be patchy outside London.

5   Some of those interviewed felt that more community groups should be resourced to provide health information and advice, including information aimed at parents and children themselves.

5 Social services provision

Asylum-seeking and refugee children have the same entitlements to assessment, protection and support from social services departments as any other child in the UK. These entitlements are outlined in the Children Act 1989 and the Children (Scotland) Act 1995. While there has been much research and lobbying about the needs of unaccompanied refugee children, the body of knowledge concerning refugee children who present themselves to social services with adult carers is entirely absent. The needs, provision and concerns about unaccompanied and accompanied children are, therefore, discussed separately.

Children with families

Asylum-seeking and refugee children have the same entitlements to protection and social care as other children in the UK. Recent case law has established that Social Services are responsible for funding community care for asylum-seekers supported by NASS, while NASS is responsible for basic levels of support.

Refugee children who are cared for by parents present themselves to social services departments, for assessment and support under the provisions of the Children Act and other relevant legislation. However, no national statistics exist that monitor refugee children's assessment outcomes, uptake and support by social services departments. It is not known whether refugee children are under-represented or over-represented in the cases assessed and supported by social services departments. Research is presently being undertaken in the London Borough of Camden after a seemingly large number of Congolese children were recorded on the local authority 'at risk' register. Research on disabled refugees also highlights an absence of data on disabled refugees, including children (Roberts and Harris, 2000). This is a clear gap in knowledge that needs to be remedied.

Focus group discussions as well as interviews with refugee communities and social services departments highlighted the following concerns:

1   Despite clear and explicit social services assessment procedures for refugee children, in some local authorities refugee children with families do not appear to be assessed using these recognised criteria. Instead, families may be seen by the local authority asylum teams. Here there is not usually a full assessment. (The Departments of Health's own internal research confirmed this in 1998.)

2   In some local authorities, interpreters are not used while assessing children within families.

3   Asylum-seeking and sometimes refugee families are told that the children and families teams of social services departments have no responsibility for them. Instead they are the responsibility of an asylum team or NASS.

4   High mobility, especially in Greater London can prevent continuity of care.

5   It was felt that a significant minority of refugee children housed in hostel accommodation were unsafe.

6   There was concern about the apparent lack of focus on the needs of refugee communities in Children's Services Plans or Quality Protects initiatives.

Many of the concerns raised in interviews have their roots in the Asylum and Immigration Act 1996. The Act resulted in social services departments being given responsibility for destitute asylum-seekers who had lost their entitlement to benefits. Some social services departments set up asylum teams that assessed and supported all destitute asylum-seekers. Other social services set up 'adult asylum teams' for adult claimants without children. Families with children were either seen by a specialist children and families asylum team or a generic children and families team. It should be noted that many staff in asylum teams were/are not social workers. Many staff were provided by agencies, so any build-up of staff expertise about refugee children was minimal. There is a marked trend in some local authorities to refer any asylum-seeker to the asylum team, irrespective of needs.

Local authority social services departments were not fully reimbursed for their support of destitute asylum-seekers after 1996 (a statutory duty). A number of local authorities were forced to make spending cuts in their non-statutory work – often amid local opposition, especially in the local media. Asylum-seekers became an unpopular local problem and arguably this has prevented local authority social services departments developing innovative and proactive work with asylum-seeking and refugee children and families.

Child protection

There is very little data or research on child protection issues among refugee communities. Research carried out by the author in 2003, showed the over-representation of Congolese children on the Child Protection Register in one London LEA. Neglect caused by parental hours of work was an issue in this local authority. Physical punishment and severe inter-generational conflict were also indicated (Rutter, 2003). Interviews highlighted issues, namely:

- Hostel accommodation may put children at risk.

- High mobility may prevent continuity of support from social services, or in the worse case children being put at risk as they move across local authority boundaries.

- Social workers' levels of awareness about refugee children's backgrounds and specific needs were often felt to be poor.

- There are some child protection issues specific to certain communities, including female genital mutilation among refugees from Africa and the Yemen, and child marriage among some eastern European Roma. Much more work needs to be carried out with community groups and community leaders in order to ensure the protection of children who may be at risk.

While Victoria Climbie was not a refugee, many of the issues raised by her tragic death are of relevance to social services departments, the police, healthcare providers and others concerned with the protection of refugee children. It is hoped that the recommendations of the inquiry into her death may also improve child protection systems for refugee children.

Unaccompanied asylum-seeking and refugee children: background and needs

The United Nations High Commissioner for Refugees (UNHCR) defines unaccompanied children as 'those who are separated from both parents and are not being cared for by an adult who, by law or custom has responsibility to do so' (UNHCR, 1994). The UN Convention on the Rights of the Child and the Children Act 1989 define a child as anyone under the age of 18 years. Using the UNHCR definition, unaccompanied refugee children include:

- children who have become separated from their parents and have arrived in the UK by themselves

- children who are being cared for by older siblings, distant relatives and family friends – therefore, not their usual carers

- children who arrived in the UK with family, other relatives or family friends but whose care arrangements break down after arrival.

In 2000 some 2,733 asylum-seeking children arrived by themselves in the UK and were identified as unaccompanied asylum-seeking children by the Immigration and Nationality Directorate of the Home Office. Casework statistics from the Refugee Council's Panel of Advisers for Unaccompanied Refugee Children indicate that most of those referred to the Panel were between 13 years and 18 years old, with less than 3 per cent of referrals being for children under 8 years old. Both statistics, however, underestimate the numbers of unaccompanied refugee children under 8 years old. This is because many refugee children cared for by older siblings, relatives or friends do not always come to the attention of the Home Office, social services or the Refugee Council.

Unaccompanied refugee children come from a variety of countries. In 2000, the main countries of origin were Afghanistan, Iraq, the Federal Republic of Yugoslavia, Somalia, Sri Lanka and Turkey. Their numbers include many more boys than girls.

The majority of the UK's unaccompanied asylum-seeking and refugee children are the responsibility of social services departments in Greater London and the South East. Kent, West Sussex, Hillingdon and Croydon support the greatest numbers of them.

Unaccompanied children have many of the same needs as other groups of refugee children, for example the need to learn English. In addition, some refugee advocates argue that unaccompanied children are the most vulnerable of refugee children, because they lack the support of a family. It should be noted that family separation or loss, however, never occur in isolation – an unaccompanied refugee child will have experienced other traumatic events, such as war.

Current provision

Central government responsibilities

British asylum law currently makes little distinction between adult and unaccompanied child asylum-seekers, although there are some concessions. At present, an unaccompanied child who does not qualify for refugee status (almost all) will be granted Discretionary Leave until their 18th birthday. No unaccompanied child has been removed from the UK since the early 1990s.

At present the Home Office is leading a review of support for unaccompanied asylum-seeking children, as a result of lobbying by local authorities in London and the South East. Some of the review process is being undertaken by the

Unaccompanied Asylum-Seeking Children Forum. The Home Office also administers the Special Grant for Unaccompanied Asylum Seeking Children, which is payable for support offered under Section 17 and Section 20 of the Children Act 1989, although not all local authorities who support such children receive it.

In England, the Department of Health coordinates the Children and Families from Overseas Network – a forum on refugee children whose membership comprises social services departments and non-governmental organisations. Its agenda has been dominated by issues about unaccompanied children. Central government has also encouraged some good practice initiatives. In 1995, the Department of Health published practice guidelines and a training pack on unaccompanied refugee children. The DfEE and the Department of Health have a published circular: *Guidance on the Education of Children Being Looked After by Local Authorities* (2000). It requires that all local authorities have a teacher or education officer who has clear responsibility for looked-after children. It also requires that looked-after children do not spend more than 20 days out of education.

Local government

The Immigration and Asylum Act 1999 makes it clear that the responsibility for unaccompanied asylum-seeking children under 18 years lies with local authority social services departments under the provisions of the Children Act 1989 and the Children (Scotland) Act 1995. No unaccompanied asylum-seeker under 18 is meant to be supported by the National Asylum Support Service. The Children Act 1989 makes a local authority social services department responsible for providing support to all children 'in need' living within its boundaries. For unaccompanied refugee children this is taken to be the local authority to which the child first presents. Consequently local authorities in London and the South East are responsible for most of the UK's unaccompanied children.

Almost all unaccompanied children under eight years old are cared for under Section 20 of the Children Act 1989. The most usual care arrangements for them are:

* *Placement with close relatives* – the children are cared for by close relatives such as siblings, aunts and uncles after they arrive in the UK. While many children are happy being cared for by close relatives, some are not and there is no statutory requirement under the Children Act for the ongoing monitoring of unaccompanied children where they are being cared for by close family. Siblings may be unaware of support offered to young carers.

- *Informal care* – many asylum-seeking and refugee children who arrive in the UK without their parents are cared for by distant relatives or family friends. Sometimes social services departments will know of informal care arrangements; in other cases they will not. Strictly speaking, this informal care should be regarded as a private foster placement by a social services department and thus subject to monitoring, but in practice this is rare. Often informal care is successful; sometimes it is not. Unaccompanied refugee children may be rejected by their carers when life gets tough in the UK. Children being cared for by siblings who are only a few years older are of particular concern. There may be the usual sibling conflicts and sometimes the younger child may not accept the authority of an older sibling. The older sibling may not know of services offered by social services that can lessen the stresses experienced by young carers.

- *Fostering* – ideally, a foster family should be of a similar ethnic and linguistic background, and receive proper support from the local authority. Although a few local authorities have invested considerable resources in recruiting foster carers from refugee communities, there is a national shortage of refugee foster families. As a result, refugee children may be placed with a foster family from the same region – for example an Eritrean family caring for a Somali child – or matched in a cruder way, according to skin colour or religion. While some cross-cultural fostering works well, research conducted in the USA and Australia shows that among refugee children there is a high level of breakdown of cross-cultural foster care.

Concerns

There has been considerable research about the quality of support offered to unaccompanied children (see, for example, Russell, 1999; Kidane, 2001; Stanley, 2001). Most of the research and lobbying has, however, concentrated on provision for older unaccompanied asylum-seeking and refugee children. Concerns raised in the research relevant to younger children include:

- A significant minority of unaccompanied refugee children have no contact with people from their own community. This problem has grown, as more children are cared for in homes and foster placements outside London.

- Little extra support is generally given to refugee children being cared for by older siblings.

- Social services departments are often unaware of children being cared for by family friends or distant relatives, and as a consequence these families are not supported.

- Access to good lawyers is another key concern: young unaccompanied asylum-seekers need a lawyer who can communicate with them as well as being a skilled asylum lawyer.

6 Non-statutory organisations

A number of non-statutory organisations provide support services for refugee parents and/or refugee children. These comprise:

- larger refugee agencies such as the Refugee Council or Refugee Action

- refugee-led community groups

- organisations that work with a range of vulnerable groups, for example the Children's Society.

Larger refugee agencies

The approach of most of the larger refugee agencies has been that of providing support for adult refugees as carers of young children. As a consequence, only a small amount of the work of the larger refugee agencies is directly targeted at young children.

The Refugee Council has employed an education adviser since 1988, with a brief of improving educational provision for children aged 0–18 years. Her work has included lobbying central and local government, supporting practice initiatives, initial and in-service training and producing publications for those working with refugee children, as well as children themselves. The education adviser has also serviced an information-sharing forum called the Steering Group on Refugee Education comprising the DfES, LEAs and non-statutory organisations involved in refugee education in London and the South East.

Action research on refugee children in the early years was undertaken with Save the Children in 1998, as a result of concerns about refugee children being under-represented in early years provision (Rutter and Hyder, 1998). This research was followed up with the targeted training of early years providers.

The Refugee Council also employs an unaccompanied children's policy adviser, located with the education adviser in its policy team. Her role has been to lobby and assist in the development of better services for unaccompanied asylum-seeking and refugee children. Since the majority of such children are above 13 years of age, the unaccompanied children's adviser has been less involved with work targeted at younger refugee children. Another key member of staff is the women's adviser, whose job it is to assist community groups, including those working solely with women, to develop services. The Refugee Council has not employed a social services adviser since 1994.

The Refugee Council undertakes some direct work with unaccompanied refugee children, running the Panel of Advisers for Unaccompanied Children – advocates who help present children's needs to the Immigration and Nationality Directorate of the Home Office, social services and other service providers. Most of its clients are aged 13 and over, although a small number are under eight years. Additionally, the Refugee Council, as well as Refugee Action, Migrant Helpline, The Refugee Arrivals Project and the Scottish Refugee Council are involved in commissioning and supporting refugee families in NASS emergency accommodation prior to dispersal. The quality of some of the emergency accommodation has attracted criticism, as has the diet offered to families and children (McLeish, 2002).

The Refugee Council, with the larger children's charities, has formed the Refugee Children's Consortium, a small network of organisations that lobby on issues concerning refugee children.

Refugee Action is another large refugee organisation working in England, offering advice for newly arrived refugees and supporting community development. It does not work directly with refugee children, although it carries out community development work with refugee women. The Refugee Arrivals Project, with bases at Heathrow and Gatwick, provides advice for new arrivals (including many families) as well as other forms of support. It has recently employed a member of staff to work with unaccompanied children, a small proportion of whom will be under eight years. Other large refugee agencies such as the Scottish Refugee Council, the Welsh Refugee Council, Refugee Education and Training Advisory Service (RETAS) and Migrant Helpline have concentrated on supporting adult refugees as carers.

Of the larger refugee agencies, the Medical Foundation for the Care of Victims of Torture undertakes the greatest proportion of direct work with refugee children. Its remit is to support those who have survived torture or other forms of organised violence. Most of its work is carried out in London. The support offered is multi-dimensional: assessments for asylum applications, basic advice, small grants, individual, family or group psychotherapy, physiotherapy, other medical interventions, art therapy, a befriending scheme for unaccompanied children and so on. The Medical Foundation also runs an extensive training programme for those who work with refugees, including teachers, early years workers and others who work with young refugee children. Most of the direct work with refugee children is located in the Children and Adolescent Psychotherapy Team.

There are several conclusions that can be drawn from the above descriptions. Refugee children's needs have a low profile in most of the large refugee agencies, with the exception of the Medical Foundation. The rationale for this is that, given scarce resources, it is much more important to support adult carers of children. Additionally, they argue, young refugee children's needs are largely met by the statutory sector.

Refugee community organisations

The Refugee Council estimated that there are over 650 active refugee community organisations in the UK, with the majority being located in Greater London. Such organisations vary in size, function, and access to funding and stability. All offer basic advice on issues such as immigration status, housing and benefits. A number also offer English language classes and careers advice. Cultural events are another common activity. Most refugee community organisations serve a specific community or ethno-linguistic groups. A small number attempt to serve all communities in the locality, acting as a forum, for example Lewisham Refugee Network.

Most refugee community organisations are located in Greater London, although some of the larger urban areas such as Manchester and Birmingham also host many such groups. However the small towns and cities, in which much dispersal accommodation is located, may only have one local refugee support group to serve all communities.

Approximately 35 groups in London are refugee women's groups – for example the Somali Refugee Women's Association. A small number of other refugee community organisations run women's activities as part of their work. Young children are frequent visitors to community organisations, but very few groups run activities specifically for them. At the time of writing only six refugee community organisations in Greater London run playgroups or parent and toddler groups.

Many community organisations run 'Saturday' schools; the Resource Centre for Mother Tongue and Supplementary Schools list 257 refugee schools in Greater London alone (Resource Unit for Supplementary and Mother Tongue Schools, 2002). Other refugee community schools are independent of community groups. Most of the schools cater for young children – an age range of 4–16 years is common in such schools. The community schools usually teach the home language; some may supplement the mainstream curriculum, teaching maths and English. Religious education, sport and cultural activities are other common activities and a small number of community schools have attached youth groups. Teachers in these schools are volunteers and the schools often have little access to innovative teaching or play materials. The schools are funded by parental donations, although a small number have secured local authority or charitable funding. Two London local authorities run training programmes for community school teachers and attach funding to participation in training programmes.

The above description raises key policy issues. First, very few community organisations run targeted projects for young refugee children. The work of even well-funded community groups is dominated by 'emergency' issues: preventing removal, securing release from detention, and securing housing and benefits. Children's needs come second to this. Those groups that do run projects for children are usually from communities where larger proportions have secure housing and immigration status.

Secondly, the agenda of some community organisations is male-dominated (Kay, 1987; Richman, 1995). Children's welfare is thus considered the prime responsibility of women and a private task, centred on the home. This again may prevent some organisations from developing projects for refugee children.

There will always be some refugees who have no contact with community groups, including many with parental responsibilities. There may be no group in their locality – an issue for many asylum-seekers dispersed by NASS. Some refugees may be unwilling to have contact with a particular group, for personal or political reasons. Those planning and delivering services for young children should, therefore, not over-rely on community groups.

Lastly, desk research, visits and discussions indicate that the links between statutory service providers and community groups are very weak. Refugee teams within education were judged to have the strongest links, while social services and early years teams had the weakest links, despite the requirement for consultation and partnership. There is no sharing of good practice on early years issues, nor are there any focused regional groups that could do this. With a few exceptions, little monies from Sure Start or the Children's Fund have enabled community groups to implement projects. If there is to be an expansion of quality early years provision and in the numbers employed as early years workers, refugees must be part of this. This necessitates much stronger partnership between local authorities and community organisations.

General children's and welfare charities

A number of children's charities, as well as charities with a general welfare remit, are working with refugee children, as well as supporting their parents. Some of these charities are large national organisations: The Children's Society, NCH Action for Children, Save the Children and Barnardo's all work with refugee children and their parents. These organisations, as well as the National Children's Bureau (NCB), have undertaken lobbying and policy work about refugee children and are part of an informal consortium.

Other organisations are smaller and work within a specific area. Many children's or welfare charities also run projects not directly targeted at refugees but whose clients are mostly refugees. Such projects include the Bayswater Centre for Homeless Families, or the Shaftesbury Society's furniture warehouse and children's toy and clothing project.

Among children's and welfare charities there is some innovative and important work with refugees. Examples include the Bayswater Centre – a centre for homeless families in central London funded by NCH Action for Children and the statutory sector. It offers a wide range of support to homeless families, most of which are refugee families, and has served as a model of good practice.

Many of the children's and general welfare organisations have been more successful than refugee community organisations in securing funding, including Children's Fund monies. However, there is a need for better sharing of good practice and networking on children's issues; smaller organisations such as Welcare, the Shaftesbury Society and Home Start are not always a part of networks.

7 Conclusions

Five policy issues emerge strongly from the research and deserve further exploration, as well as consideration by central government:

1   UK legislation and policy tends to treat asylum-seeking and refugee children as asylum-seekers and refugees first and foremost, rather than as children. Consequently, these children face restrictions to their rights and entitlements.

2   There are real discontinuities in government policy regarding asylum-seeking and refugee children. For example, while it is government policy to reduce the numbers of children living in poverty, much asylum legislation serves to increase the numbers of asylum-seeking children living in poverty.

3   Central government fails to recognise (or ignores) the fact that in many urban areas refugee children now comprise a significant minority – up to 15 per cent of all pupils in some inner London LEAs. These children's needs are not being considered in mainstream policy making, but rather as 'an add on', if at all. For example, the DfES decision to delegate more educational funding, and away from LEAs, has destroyed much central LEA support and strategic planning for refugees. This concern was made known to the DfES, but discounted, as the needs of refugee pupils were not considered great enough to reverse the funding policy.

4   There appears to be a lack of real partnership between the statutory sector (education, early years, social services and healthcare) and refugee community groups. There is much potential for partnership, for example assisting refugee groups in developing their own early years provision, but this is not happening.

5   There is much less lobbying and policy development work on refugee children's issues taking place in Wales and Scotland, as well as little evidence of diverging practice, for example in the induction and early support of asylum-seeking children in schools (Save the Children Scotland, 2002).

8 Gaps in knowledge and research and development priorities

Research issues

Research on refugees involves important ethical and methodological issues. These must be considered when planning future research. Clearly, during the course of research on refugees, a researcher may be party to a great deal of confidential information. However, all research bodies have clear guidelines about confidentiality and the maintenance of confidential records. Other ethical issues, too, impact on research on refugee children, all of which must be addressed by the researcher, namely:

- considering conflicting interests that may arise out of the research

- collaboration with refugee pressure groups who may have a particular point of view

- obtaining informed consent from refugee children and their carers – a relevant issue if the carer is suspicious of authorities or does not speak English. There is a real need to invest time and interpreting costs to explain the purpose of the research and issues about confidentiality

- avoiding excessive intrusion and stress when interviewing children. This is an issue where refugee children may be asked about prior experiences (these can include witnessing or being the victim of organised violence). If interviewed during the school day, it is good practice to ensure that there is a room where a child can sit if she/he is upset and that there are sympathetic adults or friends to hand

- ensuring refugee children's voices are represented and not relying on interviewing carers and service providers when conducting research about refugee children

- giving feedback and briefings to those who have participated or helped in the research

- working in partnership with refugee organisations to support the former with lobbying activities that may arise from the research.

Methodology

Researching refugees also raises key methodological questions. Refugees can be regarded as a special or rare population – a group that is difficult to locate and therefore difficult to sample (Sudman and Kalton, 1986 as cited in Bloch, 1999). (Other rare groups might include illegal workers or drug users.) As a result much refugee research has used snowball sampling as a method of identifying refugees for research. Carey-Wood and her colleagues used snowballing to identify refugees interviewed for Home Office research. Fieldworkers, often active in community groups, were asked to identify members of their own community (Carey-Wood *et al.*, 1995). Local authority refugee research has also used snowballing, often sampling from groups of refugees who attended community groups (Haringey, London Borough of, 1998). The shortcomings of snowball sampling are that the sampling frame is often only constructed from a small friendship network. The reliance on community group usage may also cause bias: those who use and are active in community groups may not reflect the background and needs of the whole community.

A representative sample of refugee children of school age can be achieved by constructing a sampling frame from an LEA or school enrolment data. Constructing a representative sample of refugee children under five years of age and their carers may be much more difficult.

Researching refugees also raises many cross-cultural issues (Hantrais and Mangen, 1996; Ahearn, 2000). Children and their carers may be interviewed in their home languages, or asked to fill in questionnaires. One of the major issues involved in such cross-cultural research is ensuring questions and terminology are comparable across ethno-linguistic groups. If using teams of interviewers, it is therefore a good idea to involve them in research design, including the design of questionnaire schedules. Another cross-cultural issue concerns the interpretation of ethnographic data, such as observations of groups of refugee children. The researcher may attach very different meaning to an observation from someone who is within that community. A practical solution might be to work with a researcher from the relevant community who is able to aid in the interpretation of data.

Gaps in knowledge and research priorities

In preparing this position report, a literature review was conducted. Key researchers in universities were also approached. This process itself was instructive.

The Immigration and Nationality Directorate of the Home Office supports the largest amount of research on refugee issues in the UK. Its ongoing and recent research has not focused on young children, although some of its research will be of relevance to those working with refugee children, for example, research looking at the local impact of refugees undertaken by Gary Craig at the University of Hull. The Home Office is also attempting to build links with researchers in other government departments, in order to commission joint research.

Much research on refugee children is often subsumed and intertwined with material on children from minority ethnic communities or bilingual children (see for example Bourne and Blair, 1998). It is often very difficult to extract refugee-specific data and policy from such research (Castles *et al.*, 2001).

The literature survey indicates that most research on refugee children has focused on their psychological profiles and psychiatric morbidity. However, there has been very little research that attempts to evaluate what makes a successful psychosocial intervention for a refugee child living in the UK. Other research on healthcare issues for refugee children has focused on analysing shortcomings in existing provision, or researching good practice (see McLeish, 2002; Royal College of Paediatricians, 1999).

Within education, most of the research has examined the effectiveness of existing policy and practice. Presently, research is being conducted at London Metropolitan University on the achievements and experiences of Congolese and Somali children. A doctoral student from Queen Mary and Westfield College, London is also completing research on the education of eastern European Roma asylum-seekers. The School of Education, University of Edinburgh has a proposed research project looking at refugee children's experiences of play and playgrounds.

There is a growing body of research about unaccompanied refugee children, in particular their experiences of immigration, social services assessment and support. The School of Social Work at the University of York is presently conducting research on the support offered to unaccompanied children by four case study local authorities. A clear gap in knowledge about unaccompanied children concerns their educational experiences and progression into work. There is very little published about the experiences of the social services assessment and support of refugee children with families. The School of Social Work, University of Middlesex probably has the greatest academic expertise on this issue.

Service providers within education, healthcare, social welfare, as well as NGOs, lack adequate demographic data to enable them to plan and monitor their services. At present, NASS issues health authorities and LEAs with data on asylum-seeking families living in particular areas (this data has been criticised for its reliability). The Research Division of the Immigration and Nationality Directorate is planning demographic research on refugee settlement patterns in the UK; it is hoped that these will provide useful information for service providers.

Given existing research, as well as present policy trends, the following areas may require further research:

- a national longitudinal survey about refugee children's experiences and integration

- research on the uptake of non-statutory services such as early years services and family centres

- research on the way in which refugee families use the health service

- an evaluation of the levels of English as an additional language and other support offered to refugee children

- bilingual classroom assistants and refugee children

- an evaluation of the role of citizenship education in challenging racism in schools and promoting good relationships with receiving communities

- an evaluation of mentoring projects for refugee children, and of different models of mentoring

- an evaluation of educational pathways for refugee children who arrive in the UK late in their educational careers

- achievement and underachievement among refugee children in school

- refugee children's experiences of special educational needs provision in the UK

- an evaluation of educational provision for unaccompanied refugee children and their progression into employment

- an evaluation of Sure Start projects with reference to refugees

- an evaluation of psychosocial interventions for refugee children in the UK

- an examination of the welfare of asylum-seeking children whose families are receiving the 'support only' option from NASS

- an examination of children's experiences of and welfare in accommodation centres

- refugee women's use of and experiences of refugee community groups

- children and families' experiences of assessment and support by social services departments

Given the major changes to the reception of asylum-seeking children introduced by the Nationality, Immigration and Asylum Act 2002, a major priority for research would be to evaluate the impact of accommodation centres on asylum-seeking children's education and welfare.

Key universities and non-governmental organisations with particular expertise about refugee children include:

- Education, Social Policy: University of North London – Jill Rutter, School of Education (including early years provision)

- Education: Institute of Education, University of London – Mano Candappa and Simon Warren

- Education: School of Education, University of Edinburgh – Joan Stead

- Social Service Provision: York University – Jim Wade

- Social Services Provision: Middlesex University – Ravi Kohli

- Social Policy, Social Welfare: Manchester Metropolitan University – Ed Mynott and Beth Humphries

- Social Policy and Social Welfare: University of York

- Host community responses: University of Hull – Gary Craig

- Host community responses: Goldsmith's College – Roger Hewitt

- Psychosocial intervention: University of East London – Giorgia Dona

- Psychosocial intervention, children in conflict: Refugee Studies Centre, University of Oxford – Jo Bowden

- Psychosocial intervention: Medical Foundation for the Care of Victims of Torture

There needs to be better networking and communication between academics researching refugee issues in the UK, including those researching refugee children. There is a European Association of Refugee Research, coordinated by the Centre for Research in Ethnic Relations, University of Warwick. The Information Centre on Asylum and Refugees (ICAR), Kings College, London also aims to coordinate and disseminate research about refugees. A useful intervention would be to run a seminar about research on refugee children.

Innovation and development

Research about refugee children by agencies with a commitment to social justice should be a starting point for lobbying by refugee and children's agencies, as well as the development of innovatory projects to support this group.

The Refugee Council, the Medical Foundation, and the large national children's agencies are the organisations presently engaged in most lobbying for refugee children. They meet as the Refugee Children's Consortium. It is important to feed back the research findings to these groups, as well as involve them in discussion about the strategic development of the Joseph Rowntree Foundation's work.

Also believed to be important is the involvement of some of the smaller agencies that work with refugee children in feedback and consultation, including some of the more established community groups.

Innovatory projects that support refugee children must not duplicate the responsibilities of statutory services. Projects should pioneer new ways of working and new activities. Projects should be evaluated, and their successes and failures disseminated via existing networks.

As a result of interview and focus group discussion, projects that the Joseph Rowntree Foundation might consider include:

- funding projects to develop cooperation in providing services to young refugee children at a regional, consortium or inter-local authority level

- training in conducting needs analysis for refugee community organisations and agencies. With some notable exceptions, much research conducted by larger and smaller refugee agencies has not been of high quality

- a programme of work that would enable refugee community organisations to set up their own early years projects – whether a nursery or playgroup

- developing innovative approaches to supporting refugee children by educational psychology services

- developing innovative approaches to supporting refugee children by setting up children and families teams within social services departments, with strong emphasis on disseminating good practice

- supporting Somali teachers, mentors, classroom assistants, early years workers, other educators and social care workers in their role and professional development.

References

Ahearn, F. (ed.) (2000) *The Psychological Wellness of Refugees: Issues in Qualitative and Quantitative Research*. New York: Berghahn Books

Ahearn, F. and Athey, J. (eds) (1991) *Refugee Children: Theory, Research and Services*. Baltimore: John Hopkins University Press

Ali, E. and Jones, C. (2000) *Meeting the Educational Needs of Somali Pupils in Camden Schools*. London: London Borough of Camden

Arshad, R., Closs, A. and Stead, J. (1999) *Doing Our Best: Scottish School Education, Refugee Pupils and Parents – a strategy for social inclusion*. Edinburgh: Centre for Education in Racial Equality in Scotland

Bloch, A. (1999) 'Carrying out a Survey of Refugees: some methodological considerations and guidelines', *Journal of Refugee Studies*, Vol. 12, No. 4, pp. 367–83

Bourne, J. and Blair, M. (1998) *Making the Difference: Teaching and Learning Strategies in Successful Multi-ethnic Schools*. London: DfEE

Burnett, A. and Fassil, Y. (2002) *Meeting the Health Needs of Refugees and Asylum-seekers in the UK*. London: London Directorate for Health and Social Care

Camden, London Borough of (1996) *Refugee Education Policy*, unpublished report

Candappa, M. (2000) 'Extraordinary childhoods: the social lives of refugee children', ESCR Research Briefing 5

Carey-Wood, J., Duke, K., Karn, V. and Marshall, T. (1995) *The Settlement of Refugees in Britain*. London: Home Office Research Study 141, HMSO

Castles, S., Korac, M., Vasta, E. and Vertovec, S. (2001) *Integration: Mapping the Field*. London: Home Office

Community Health South London NHS Trust (2001) *The Needs of Young Refugees in Lambeth, Southwark and Lewisham*, unpublished research report

Community Relations Commission (1976) *Refuge or Home? A Policy Statement on the Resettlement of Refugees*. London: CRC

Daycare Trust (2002) *Meeting the Child Poverty Challenge*, Policy Paper 3. London: Daycare Trust

Department for Education and Skills (2002) *Guidance on the Education of Asylum-seeking and Refugee Children*. London: DfES

DfEE/Department of Health (2000) *Guidance on the Education of Children Being Looked After by Local Authorities*. London: DfEE/Department of Health

Dobson, J., Henthorne, K. and Lynas, Z. (2000) *Pupil Mobility in Schools.* London: Migration Research Unit, University College London

Dorkenoo, E. and Ellworthy, S. (1994) *Female Genital Mutilation: Proposals for Change.* London: Minority Rights Group

European Commission (2001) Proposal from the European Commission for a Council Directive Laying Down Minimum Standards for Their Reception of Applicants for Asylum (Com. 2001 No. 181, Brussels, European Commission)

Greater London Authority (2001) *Refugees and Asylum-Seekers in London: a GLA Perspective.* London: GLA

Greater London Authority (2002, forthcoming) *Sold Short: Resource Issues and Refugee Children's Education.* London: GLA

Hantrais, L. and Mangen, S. (eds) (1996) *Cross National Research Methods in the Social Sciences.* London: Pinter

Haringey, London Borough of (1998) *Refugees in Haringey.* London: London Borough of Haringey

Home Office (1997) *Asylum Statistics 1996.* London: Home Office

Home Office (2002a) 'Asylum Statistics, 2002', unpublished report available on www.homeoffice.gov.uk

Home Office (2002b) *Secure Borders, Safe Havens: Integration with Diversity in Modern Britain* (White Paper). London: Home Office

Kay, D. (1987) *Chileans in Exile: Private Struggles, Public Lives.* London: Macmillan

Kidane, S. (2001) *I Did Not Choose to Come Here: Listening to Refugee Children.* London: BAAF

London Research Centre (1999) *Homelessness in London,* Bulletin 15. London: London Research Centre

McLeish, J. (2002) *Mothers in Exile: the Maternity Experiences of Asylum Seekers in England.* London: Maternity Alliance

Mott, G. (2000) *Refugees and Asylum-seekers: the Role of LEAs.* Slough: EMIE

Norton, R. and Cohen, B. (2000) *Out of Exile: Developing Youth Work with Young Refugees.* London: National Youth Agency

OFSTED (2000) *Evaluating Inclusion: Guidance for Inspectors and Schools.* London: OFSTED

OFSTED and the Audit Commission (2001) *Local Education Authority Support for Schools in Inner London.* London: OFSTED

Power, S., Whitty, G. and Youdell, D. (1998) 'Refugees, asylum-seekers and the housing crisis: no place to learn', in J. Rutter and C. Jones (eds) *Refugee Education: Mapping the Field.* Stoke on Trent: Trentham Books

Refugee Council (2000) *Helping Refugee Children in Schools.* London: Refugee Council

Refugee Council (2002) *A Case for Change: How Refugee Children in England Are Missing Out.* London: Refugee Council

Refugee Council and Oxfam (2002) *Poverty and Asylum in the UK.* London: Refugee Council

Resource Unit for Supplementary and Mother Tongue Schools (2002) *Directory of Supplementary and Mother Tongue Classes 2002.* London: RUSMS

Richman, N. (1995) 'They don't recognise our dignity', a study of young refugees in the London Borough of Hackney, unpublished report, City and Hackney Community NHS Trust

Roberts, K. and Harris, J. (2000) *Disabled Refugees and Asylum-Seekers in Britain: Numbers and Social Characteristics.* York: University of York Social Policy Research Unit

Robinson, V. and Hale, S. (1989) *The Geography of Vietnamese Secondary Migration in the UK,* Research Paper 10. Warwick: Centre for Research in Ethnic Relations

Royal College of Paediatricians (1999) *The Health of Refugee Children; Guidelines for Paediatricians.* London: Royal College of Paediatricians

Russell, S. (1999) *Most Vulnerable of All: the Treatment of Unaccompanied Children in the UK.* London: Amnesty International (UK)

Rutter, J. (1999) 'An analysis of OFSTED inspections of Greater London secondary schools', unpublished research, Refugee Council

Rutter, J. (2001) *Supporting Refugee Children in 21st Century Britain.* Stoke on Trent: Trentham Books. Second edition 2002

Rutter, J. (2003) *The Experiences and Achievements of Congolese Children in Camden Schools.* London: London Borough of Camden

Rutter, J. and Hyder, T. (1998) *Refugee Children in the Early Years.* London: Refugee Council and Save the Children

Rutter, J. and Stanton, R. (2001) 'Refugee children's education and the educational finance system', *Multicultural Teaching*, Vol. 19, No. 3

Save the Children (1997) Lets Spell It Out: Peer Research by the Horn of Africa Youth Scheme. London: Save the Children

Save the Children and the Refugee Council (2001) *In Safe Hands: A Video Training Pack for those Working with Young Refugee Children*. London: Save the Children/ Refugee Council

Save the Children, Scotland (2002) *Starting Again*. Glasgow: Save the Children, Scotland

Sellen, D., Tedstone, A. and Frize, J. (2000) 'Research development: young refugee children's diets and family coping strategies in East London', unpublished final report from the Public Health Nutrition Unit, London School of Hygiene and Tropical Medicine

Stanley, K. (2001) *Cold Comfort: Young Separated Refugees in England*. London: Save the Children

Sudman, S. and Kalton, G. (1986) 'New developments in the sampling of special populations', *Annual Review of Sociology*, Vol. 31, No. 3, pp. 607–18

UNHCR (1994) *Refugee Children: Guidelines on Protection and Care*. Geneva: UNHCR

Appendix

Table A1.1 Asylum-seeking and refugee children in UK schools 1989–2001

Country of origin	Total asylum applications 1989–2001, excluding dependants	Notes
Afghanistan	26,015	
Albania	3,895 (since 1999)	Most applicants have arrived since 1999
Algeria	10,190	
Angola	12,535	
Bosnia	An estimated 8,000 asylum applications were lodged by Bosnians. The UK also accepted those evacuated from Croatia as part of the Bosnia programme	Peak years of application 1992–1995
Bulgaria	Less than 1,000	
Burundi	Less than 1,000	
Cameroon	Less than 1,000	
Colombia	6,620	Other Colombians have fled violence and are living in the UK, but have not applied for asylum
Croatia	An estimated 3,000 asylum applicants	Numbers include those fleeing in 1991 who have been unable to return to their homes
Czech Republic	4,755	Most applications made after 1998. Almost all the asylum applicants are Roma. Less than 1 per cent are granted refugee status or ELR
Democratic Republic of Congo	19,035	
Congo–Brazzaville	Less than 1,000	
Eritrea	An estimated 11,000	Eritrean asylum applications were included with those from Ethiopia until June 1993
Ethiopia	An estimated 13,000, with 1,480 applications 1999–2001	
India	22,115	Less than 1 per cent of applicants from India were granted refugee status or ELR. There are very few children among Indian asylum applicants
Iran	15,535	Many Iranians also arrived in the period after the 1979 Revolution
Iraq	24,205	Figure also includes those who have fled the Kurdish autonomous area (mostly Kurds and Assyrians)
Ivory Coast	4,400	Peak year of application was 1991
Kenya	7,020	
Lebanon	3,694	Peak years of application were 1990 and 1991
Liberia	Less than 2,000	
Nigeria	21,265	Less than 2 per cent of applicants have been granted refugee status or ELR

Continued

Table A1.1 Asylum-seeking and refugee children in UK schools 1989–2001 *(Cont'd)*

Country of origin	Total asylum applications 1989–2001, excluding dependants	Notes
Pakistan		
Poland	8,480	Almost all the asylum applicants are Roma. Very few are granted refugee status or ELR
Romania	10,325	The majority (although not all) asylum applicants are Roma. Very few are granted refugee status or ELR
Sierra Leone	10,315	
Somalia	42,640	The largest recently arrived refugee community in the UK. At least 15,000 Somalis have also arrived after gaining refugee status (or naturalisation) in other EU countries. Total community in UK estimated to be 180,000.
Sri Lanka	41,100	
Sudan	4,310	
Turkey	28,055	
Uganda	8,710	
Vietnam	Over 25,000	They have arrived on the three Refugee Programmes (1979–84, 84–88, 88–92), or through the Orderly Departure Programme or as asylum-seekers
Yugoslavia	An estimated 22,000 applicants plus those who arrived on the Bosnia Programme	Asylum applicants from Serbia, Kosova and Montenegro
Zimbabwe	3,325	Very few asylum applicants before 2000. Zimbabweans now make up one of the largest groups arriving in the UK

Table A1.2 Asylum seekers supported by NASS in regions, as at end of March 2003

Government Office Region	In receipt of subsistence only	Supported in NASS accommodation
North East	250	5,865
North West	1,125	10,165
Yorks and Humberside	905	10,320
East Midlands	1,275	4,375
West Midlands	1,430	9,940
East of England	1,410	540
Greater London	28,345	2,770
South East	2,500	1,185
South West	600	1,005
Wales	185	1,870
Scotland	350	6,070
Northern Ireland	25	180

Source: Home Office. Asylum Statistics available on www.homeoffice.gov.uk

Table A1.3 Refugee children in Greater London schools, January 2002

LEA	Dec 1998 refugee numbers	Jan 2002 refugee numbers	Total pupil numbers	Refugees as a % of pupil numbers	Notes
Barking and Dagenham	143 children	964 refugee children	28,916 total pupils	3.3	The largest groups are Kosovars and Congolese. This LEA employed two refugee support teachers until 1999, after which English language and refugee support were devolved to schools
Barnet	2,176	1,315	47,109	2.8	Main groups: Iranians, Somalis, Kurds and Tamils English language service fully devolved to schools. A New to Schooling project, working mostly with refugee children closed down when EMAG support was devolved
Bexley	65	600	39,479	1.5	The LEA employs a refugee support teacher
Brent	3,300	3,678	37,335	12% of nursery roll, 10% of primary and secondary school roll, 9% of special school roll	Main groups: Somalis, Iraqis, Afghans and Kosovars English language service devolved, but LEA has maintained a refugee education officer
Bromley	153	250	46,591	0.54	The LEA employs a refugee support teacher
Camden	1,641	2,057	22,709	9.0	Main groups: Somalis and Albanian speakers The LEA employs a refugee support team, funded by EMAG and the LEA
Croydon	807	987	48,653	2	13 per cent of all the refugee children are unaccompanied The LEA employs two refugee education advisers
Ealing	2,246	3,738	41,440	9	Main groups: Somalis and Afghans There is no refugee education specialist employed by the LEA
Enfield	1,909	1,218	47,276	2.6	Main groups: Turkish Kurds, Somalis and Tamils
Greenwich	2,057	1,662	34,907	4.8	The largest group are Somalis The LEA employs an early years refugee specialist

continued

Table A1.3 Refugee children in Greater London schools, January 2002 (*continued*)

LEA	Dec 1998 refugee numbers	Jan 2002 refugee numbers	Total pupil numbers	Refugees as a % of pupil numbers	Notes
Hackney	2,211	2,289	25,877	8.9	Main groups: Turkish Kurds The LEA employs one refugee education coordinator
Hammersmith and Fulham	782	1,486	17,248	8.6	The largest group are Somalis The LEA employs a refugee support teacher
Haringey	3,939	5,620	33,321	16.9	Main groups: Turkish Kurds, Somalis The LEA employs a refugee support team, as well as parental outreach workers specific to certain communities
Harrow	1,050	1,952	28,435	6.8	The largest group are Somalis
Havering	12	36	36,622	0.1	
Hillingdon	360	681 refugees	39,966	1.7	A large proportion of Hillingdon's refugee children are unaccompanied
Hounslow	1,382	2,462	35,014	7.0	The main groups are Somalis, Iranians, Afghans and Tamils
Islington	2,217	3,228	23,630	13.7	The main groups are Turkish Kurds and Somalis The LEA employs a refugee coordinator
Kensington and Chelsea	735	1,326	10,990	12.0	The LEA employs two refugee support teachers
Kingston	138	489	20,100	2.4	Main group: Tamils, with the increase in numbers mainly due to larger numbers of Tamils The LEA employs a refugee support teacher
Lambeth	716	1,420	27,575	5.2	
Lewisham	2,618	4,934	34,406	14.3	Increase due to increased number of Sri Lankan Tamils and Zimbabweans The LEA employs a part-time teacher for new arrivals and also funds a new arrivals worker who is employed by a refugee organisation

continued

Table A1.3 Refugee children in Greater London schools, January 2002 (continued)

LEA	Dec 1998 refugee numbers	Jan 2002 refugee numbers	Total pupil numbers	Refugees as a % of pupil numbers	Notes
Merton	2,419	1,900	22,379	8.5	The LEA employs a refugee support teacher
Newham	4,279	5,689	47,646	12.6	Main groups: Somalis, Somali Bravanese The LEA has a large refugee support team comprising teachers and home school liaison workers
Redbridge	1,018	2,175	41,978	5.2	The LEA employs a refugee support teacher
Richmond	178	216	19, 358	1.1	Over 45 per cent are Afghans
Southwark	2,900	1,248	34,446	3.6	
Sutton	96	210	27,259	0.7	
Tower Hamlets	1,118	1,919	36,752	5.2	The main group is Somalis, the LEA employs a specialist adviser to work with them
Waltham Forest	1,100	2,500 estimate based on admissions	34,706	7.2	The LEA emplys a refugee adviser
Wandsworth	950	1,903	27,994	6.8	The largest group are Tamils The LEA employs a refugee support teacher
Westminster	2,478	2,514	18,130	13.9	

Total refugee children in Greater London, December 1998 = 47,193
Total refugee children in Greater London, January 2002 = 62,666
Total roll (primary, secondary, special and pupil referral unit) Greater London, January 2001 = 1,038,247
Refugee children as a percentage of total school roll = 6.04%

Notes on the survey of refugee pupil numbers

The largest group of refugees in Greater London schools are children born in Somalia (including the Bravanese minority). Other large groups are Afghans, Sri Lankan Tamils, Turkish Kurds, Congoese (Zaireans) and Iranians.

The statistics on refugee numbers were gathered in December 2001. As the statistics were not gathered on the same day, there is room for error. The general pupil numbers were collected on Form Seven day in January 2001.

In some local education authorities, refugee surveys were carried out in schools by asking if students were asylum-seekers or refugees. This method tends to under-estimate refugee numbers. In other local authorities statistics were collected by analysing language surveys, and cross referencing information with Home Office data, census data and information from community groups on the size of certain communities, such as Arabic speaking countries, Nigeria, Ghana and Turkey/Cyprus.

Vietnamese children were included in the survey. Although a proportion of Vietnamese children, particularly in primary schools, have now been born in the UK, the Vietnamese are judged to be a vulnerable community. Among Vietnamese parents there are low levels of fluency in English and high unemployment. Research in process at the University of North London also indicates that the Vietnamese may be underachieving in schools.

Major demographic changes since the survey was carried out by the Refugee Council in December 1998 include:

* secondary migration back to Greater London of families dispersed by local authorities and NASS

* by an increase in the number of Sri Lankan Tamil children entering the school system.